ALASKA CALLS

Dedicated to my Husband
Stewart, without whom these
experiences would not have happened

ALASKA CALLS

VIRGINIA LECHELT NEELY

hancock

house

ISBN 0-88839-970-7
Copyright © 1983 Virginia Lechelt Neely

Catalog in Publication Data

Neely, Virginia Lechelt
Alaska calls

ISBN 0-88839-970-7

1. Neely, Virginia Lechelt. 2. Alaska — Biography. 3.
Fishermen — Alaska — Biography. I. Title.
F909.N43   979.8'04'0924   C83-091221-5

Edited by Diana Ottosen
Typeset by Elizabeth Grant in Times Roman
   on an AM Varityper Comp/Edit
Layout & Cover Design by Eva Raidl
Production by Stephanie Legault
Printed in Canada by Friesen Printers

Hancock House Publishers Ltd.

19313 Zero Ave., Surrey, B.C. Canada V3S 5J9

Hancock House Publishers Inc.

1431 Harrison Avenue, Blaine, WA, U.S.A. 98230

Table of Contents

1

Alaska!

I was awakened by something slowly rolling back and forth across the floor. Then I felt a gentle rocking motion and was aware of the muffled throb of a motor somewhere.

Where was I? Not fully awake yet I couldn't grasp the meaning of these baffling movements and sounds. Then I opened my eyes to the unfamiliar sight of a bunk bed above me and a tiny dimly-lighted room. I turned my head and saw daylight through a round window. Then I remembered! Alaska! The round window was a porthole and we were on a boat to Alaska!

It was April 1939. My younger sister and I, both in our early twenties, had operated a small restaurant at a resort on Naches Pass highway in Washington for a year. Business wasn't very good but we worked hard and saved all we could. Ever since I was ten I had read books by Jack London and James Oliver Curwood. The north country appealed to me and I was determined to go to Alaska. When my sister agreed to go with me we gathered all the information we could about the territory, which wasn't much and not all accurate.

Finally we bought tickets on the small freighter *Tongass*, of the Alaska Transportation Company. It carried only twelve passengers. Our destination was Juneau, simply because it was the farthest north our finances would allow us to travel. This was also the reason we were going on a freighter instead of on one of the much faster and larger Alaska Steamship Company's passenger ships. Our bank-rolls consisted of about $100 each, our tickets cost near twenty dollars each. No one in our small town had ever been to the Territory of Alaska, presumably a land of ice and snow, Eskimos and igloos. So amid a mixture of well-wishes

6

and sad goodbyes we left our hometown of Kennewick, Washington, traveling by bus to Seattle. The anticipation of my long dreamed-of trip was somewhat tempered by the uncertainty and anxiety as to what lay ahead.

Arriving in Seattle early in the evening we went directly to the dock and were allowed to go aboard although the freighter would not sail until one A.M. After investigating our cabin which had two bunks, one over the other, and a small wash basin, we hung clothes on the few hangers we found at the foot of the bunks. Other things were left in suitcases we pushed under the bunk. Then, fascinated by the glow and sparkle of the night-lights of the biggest city we had ever seen, we stood on the deck and watched the activity and listened to the strange noise and sounds along the waterfront. Trucks rumbled onto docks, taxis honked, crewmen and longshoremen shouted as boats were loaded or unloaded. The clanging of machinery was interspersed with the laughter of youngsters on bicycles.

By 9:30 we were tired and sleepy from the long bus ride and being country girls we went to bed. No other passengers had come aboard yet. We learned later that going to bed early just wasn't the thing to do, as everyone comes on shortly before departure time in various states of bon voyage merrymaking and stands at the rail waving and shouting goodbyes to friends and relatives as the ship casts off.

We slept through it all.

"Fern, wake up! We're on the way!" I excitedly called to my sister as I clambered out of bed and gave the blanket in the upper bunk a tug.

Fern awakened and joined me at the porthole. Soon we were dressed and out on the deck. I breathed deeply of the damp salt air, so different from the dry air of eastern Washington. We spoke to the only other person outside, a young lady about my age with long dark hair. She told us she was Helen Harper, from Montana, and was going to Juneau first but intended to go on to Anchorage to homestead some land. Amazed at her daring ambition we questioned her further and learned that in her baggage she had an axe, saw and other tools. Although she was tall and well proportioned, she didn't appear to be the rugged type one would expect to see going into the wilderness alone. I wondered how she ever had the courage to strike out alone since it was immediately apparent that she was painfully shy; especially in the presence of men she stood mute with downcast eyes.

"Let's go to breakfast Fern. Coming Helen?" I said as the gong sounded. We gathered in the small dining room with others,

7

six on each side of a table with raised edges. A steward served the meals such as one might be served in an average cafe, but with limited choice. To me it was luxury to be served three meals a day and walk away without any dishwashing.

There we met the other passengers. There was a middle-aged couple, both considerably overweight, who drank and quarreled all the way to Juneau; a younger couple, quiet but friendly, hoping to get rich quickly; a red-headed woman with so much make-up on she looked like a wax doll, being just about as cold and expressionless. I understood her appearance better when I learned she was an inhabitant of South Franklin Street, the red-light district. There were two miners going back to the Alaska-Juneau gold mine after a vacation "Outside" and an Englishman, Harvey Moore. He was a strong-looking husky six-footer, perhaps forty-five, an old timer in Alaska with an English accent, going back to Juneau as foreman on a road-building project. He was sharp-eyed and alert, yet quiet and unassuming with a dry sense of humor. As we became better acquainted he gave us three girls much information about Alaska, spiced with a few obviously tall tales.

The regular passenger ships made the trip to Juneau in three or four days but it was an eight-day trip for our slower ship, with stops of several hours in Ketchikan, Wrangell and Petersburg while unloading freight. We enjoyed everything, particularly the heavily wooded green forests and lush foliage that came right down to the beach. In the background were snow-covered mountains, the increasingly lower snow-line ever reminding us that we were traveling north. We watched porpoises racing beside the boat and at times saw whales spouting steam into the crisp air.

The boat often passed between pretty little islands, sometimes so close we could have tossed a stone from the deck to the island. I never tired of watching the sea, sometimes a deep blue and other times a bright green. Some days it was so smooth and clear that the clouds were reflected in the water as if in a mirror until a breeze or riptide stirred up choppy waves and the pictures disappeared. Only once, when crossing Dixon Entrance, a stretch of open sea not sheltered by islands, did it get quite rough and Fern and I learned what it meant to be seasick. We solved this by taking to our bunks until we were once again in smooth waters.

Everyone went ashore while freight was being unloaded. Some spent most of the time in the saloons and were barely able to stagger aboard by departure time. My sister and I always invited Helen to go with us, visiting the gift shops and looking at the displays of handicraft wares the Indian women had arranged on blankets spread on the sidewalk. There were moccasins of all sizes made from seal skins and trimmed with colorful glass beads. Baskets, beaded belts and necklaces were among other items for sale.

"What kind of material do you use to make these?" I asked, examining a small basket of interesting design.

"We make with strips we peel off the inside of cedar bark," an elderly Indian answered. A flicker of expectancy moved across the dark face lined with deep wrinkles. Wisps of gray hair escaped from beneath the faded scarf on her head. "You like?" she asked.

"Come on," Fern whispered, giving my sleeve a tug. "We can't afford anything." Reluctantly I moved on.

During each stop-over Harvey Moore invariably showed up at an opportune moment with a hearty "How 'aboot' coffee and doughnuts, then I'll show you the town." This usually wouldn't take long. At that time Wrangell had a population of about 1500, Petersburg around 2000 and Ketchikan near 3500. Wrangell and Petersburg had cement sidewalks through the main part of town but the streets were unpaved. The harbors were crowded with fishing boats, their poles pointing skyward. The many vessels were evidence of the principal means of livelihood.

Good weather favored us most of the trip but it was raining when the *Tongass* steamed up Gastineau Channel and tied up to the dock in Juneau at three in the morning. From the porthole we could see the beautiful lights of the Alaska-Juneau Gold Mine on the steep slope of what we learned was Mt. Roberts. Harvey had suggested that Helen, Fern and I stay aboard until morning, then he would help us with our baggage. We had been warned hotel rooms would be hard to find except at the largest and most expensive hotel in town because of the spring influx of job seekers. We couldn't afford a hotel room of any kind for very long.

So we *cheechakoes* (which is the Indian word for 'greenhorns') were relieved when Harvey came for us in a cab with a cheery, "Good morning, girls. Had a bit of luck this morning. My friend who owns the Alaskan Hotel was 'aboot' out of rooms when I asked him to save two for you girls."

It was only a few blocks to a small modest carry-your-own baggage-type hotel. There was a barroom along one side of the lobby but by this time we had observed that almost every other door in these Alaskan towns led to a bar so we weren't too disturbed. We were reassured by the warm friendly way everyone greeted Harvey. Still we felt some apprehension as our new friend picked up a couple of suitcases and started up the stairs. The hotel

9

clerk came over to help, but as he reached for one of Helen's bags she snatched it away from him and with a frightened look on her face said, "I can carry my own." We were all reassured when we later learned that Harvey had given up his own room for us and had bunked with a friend.

I remember our first night in Juneau. Sharing a double bed, Fern and I lay listening to the steady drip of the rain on the roof. Home seemed thousands of miles away. The juke box in the saloon, one floor directly below us, was going full blast all night, playing mostly Scandinavian schottisches and polkas. One recording especially, a sad tale of love lost, was played over and over.

"Some Swede miner must be feeling mighty low," I grumbled.

The bursts of laughter and sometimes profane talk which we could hear in spite of the juke box did nothing to cheer us up. We slept restlessly.

The next day Helen answered an ad in the local paper and two days later she went to work as housekeeper in the home of a businessman. After three days in the hotel, Fern and I rented a sleeping-room from a friendly couple who managed the second floor of a building on the main street. We felt lucky to find a vacancy renting for much less money than the three dollars a day hotel-room. Again our room was located over a barroom. After paying a week's rent at one dollar a day, we emptied our purses on the bed and found our financial assets amounted to $24.32. Both too shaken to speak for a minute, we stared at the pitiful little pile of bills and coins.

Fern finally broke the silence, "What will we do if we don't find work?"

"We can always scrub floors," I answered, a feeble joke that fell flat. "But I'm sure we'll find something better soon." I tried to sound more optimistic than I felt.

We soon learned that jobs were not as plentiful as we had believed. The Alaska-Juneau mine, usually referred to as the A.J., provided the largest payroll in the city. There was also a significant number of government employees in Juneau, being the capital of Alaska. However, the prospects of employment attracted many people north in the depression years, and as a result there was no shortage of help. The opening of the fishing season in the spring however, absorbed many of the job seekers.

"Looks like we'll have to tighten our belts even more," Fern said as we lunched on cold pork and beans and bread in our room. Other times a large bowl of soup at a restaurant proved adequate. For breakfast a cup of coffee and a bowl of hot cereal were both satisfying and inexpensive. Our landlady never knew how much we appreciated it when she invited us for dinner one evening.

Mornings we would walk the streets looking for "help wanted" signs in the windows of stores and restaurants.

"Let's go to the library every day and look at the ads in the local paper," Fern suggested.

Sunday mornings we went to church, which was our usual custom, but now we were also anxious to meet more people, hoping some bit of casual information might prove helpful.

Afternoons we explored the seaport crowded between Gastineau Channel and snow-capped mountains. Strolling along the waterfront we would watch the ships come in and the activity in the small-boat harbor; a constant shuffling of vessels of all descriptions.

Many of the buildings along the docks and in the downtown area were old and weathered, a few having been there since before the turn of the century. Houses were a mixture of old and new, made of wood; I saw no log houses.

While searching for work we met Harvey's old friend and buddy, Neil Gallagher, a tobacco-chewing Irishman of slight but wiry build, with a constant twinkle in his blue eyes. About sixty-five, full of boundless energy and good humor, he enjoyed life, people and even a good fight after which he would admit blithely, "Some son-of-a-gun lowered the boom on me." He couldn't talk without swearing but was always good for a handout to some unfortunate person or would willingly bail someone out of jail who had indulged too freely the night before.

Every day while my sister and I looked for work, Neil and Harvey would just happen to be on the street near our room about meal-time and when we came down one or the other would hail us with "We were just going over to Percy's Cafe to eat, come along with us." They would always refuse to let us pay for our own meals. They were great company, always making fun of each other. We became good friends.

Not until months later did we learn that ever since the day Harvey had taken us to the Alaskan Hotel, Helen, Fern and I had been dubbed "Harvey's Harem" by his friends. Only then did I realize what a sensation it must have created at the hotel when this middle-aged bachelor came up on the boat from Outside with three girls in tow. He must have been teased unmercifully, however thoroughly enjoying every minute of it.

Within two weeks of our arrival, Fern went to work in a

bakery wrapping bread and waiting on customers. Two days later I was happy to find an opening for a waitress in a small bus-depot cafe. The bus carried the miners on three shifts to and from the A.J. mine day and night. It also provided transportation for anyone wanting to travel the road out of town and for people living in the country. Some travellers worked in town and some were fishermen. A week later the owner asked if I would consider being her partner in the business so the two of us could share the cooking. It meant putting in longer hours than the normal eight-hour shift. I became her partner for seventy-five dollars which she loaned me. There was no written agreement, no questions asked or references required. Surely this was the land of opportunity.

To accommodate the bus schedule the cafe was open from 5:30 A.M. to midnight. For a lunch of soup, meat, potatoes, vegetable, bread and coffee we charged forty-five cents. A cube steak was ten cents more. My partner worked from 5:00 A.M. until 2:00 P.M. when I relieved her and worked until I closed up shortly after midnight. A waitress worked a day shift. Soon after our first payday, Fern and I rented a ground-floor apartment for twenty-five dollars a month. We had a good view of the harbor and Gastineau Channel so didn't mind the eight-block walk up a steep street to our home.

Because of our different work schedules, Fern, Helen and I found little time to get together. Occasionally we did manage to hike up the trail on Mt. Roberts just behind the city or along Gold Creek and up the Basin Road. A ride in the country was limited to the bus schedule unless one was lucky enough to have a friend with a car, but relatively few people in Juneau owned a car in the thirties.

Movies were well attended; the midnight preview was especially enjoyed by those who worked the odd shifts. Occasionally, Harvey or Neal, or both, would show up at the cafe about midnight and invite me to the cinema.

It was a diversion that helped to make Juneau's annual ninety-two inch rainfall more tolerable. Surprisingly, just a few miles beyond the city limits and out of range of 4000-foot Mt. Juneau and Mt. Roberts at Juneau's back-door, the rainfall was only about half as much. Boating, hunting and fishing were favorite outdoor sports in spite of the rain.

"One of the boys that comes to the cafe is coming by in his car this morning and will take us out to the glacier," I told Fern on a Sunday that I didn't work. The Alaska Coastal Airlines hangars were located a short distance from the cafe and the fellows who worked there were regular coffee-up customers.

During the thirteen-mile ride on a gravel road we passed scattered houses, some old and others modern. Cows on a dairy farm grazed in a large meadow with mountains and a small glacier in the background. Nine miles out, at Duck Creek, we left the gravel road and followed a dirt road to Mendenhall Glacier where we gazed in amazement at this gigantic blue-green spectacle. We followed a trail along one edge of the glacier to where we could have our pictures taken sitting on the ice. On our return we stopped in clearings where blue lupine grew in abundance surrounded by spruce and hemlock trees. We gathered arms full of fuzzy-topped, long-stemmed plants known as Alaska Cotton.

"I'm leaving for Anchorage tomorrow," Helen informed Fern and I one day in late July.

"Tomorrow?" We expressed our surprise in unison.

"Yes," she explained briefly. "That's where I was headed for and I want to get settled before winter comes."

Fern took her lunch-hour early the next day and we saw Helen off at the dock. She stood at the railing as the steamship moved slowly out of the harbor and as I waved to her I felt a bit of envy for her determination and aggressiveness in pursuing her ambitious goal. I was aware of the same consuming urge to go farther north, into distant and unknown country.

With the coming of autumn and almost steady rain, the days became shorter and more dreary but no one seemed to mind. Work, schedules and activities went on just the same. I would have liked more time to see the country out of town, but even though I sometimes wearied of the long hours on the job, I found the work and the people I met interesting. Even the rainy days did nothing to diminish the thrill of the realization of my long dreamed-of venture into the north.

"What happened?" I stammered one night when we both stumbled out of bed from a sound sleep at the sudden blare of an unearthly sound I have never heard before or since.

"It must be the fire horn," Fern finally gasped, still trembling. Then we remembered we had been warned about the unusual fire alarm, but we had never dreamed of anything like this.

"It's a volunteer fire department," someone had told us, "and there's no chance anyone will fail to hear the alarm."

To me it sounded like a bellowing cow in distress amplified ten thousand times. The efficiency of the fire department was undisputed for Juneau had never had a fire that wiped out more than one building. Many Alaskan communities, which are built

13

entirely of wood materials, had been all but wiped out by fires.

The dreaded Taku wind was always a fire threat, occurring not often, but more so in the winter. The wind howled and seemed to gust from every direction with tremendous power; it was impossible to find a sheltered side of a building.

"I have a cab out here to take you home," Harvey said late one such stormy night while he struggled to pull the door to the bus depot shut. The wind had almost ripped it from his grasp. As the cab moved slowly up the hill we saw things flying through the air. The roof of a garage was blown completely off but we saw no sign of it anywhere. One person was trying to stand upright and walk by clinging to the side of a building and another actually crawled across the street. Harvey helped me to the door and saw me safely inside before going back to the waiting cab. I turned and started to remove my raincoat but stopped short when I saw Fern sitting with bruised and scratched knees. One hand was bandaged.

"What happened to you?" I asked in alarm.

"I was walking home in the middle of the street because I was afraid of getting blown off the sidewalk, when all of a sudden a gust blew me forward and I fell in the gravel," she explained.

"Are you hurt bad?" I asked.

"No," she answered. "My knees are bruised and sore but the scratches aren't deep; ruined my stockings. Got a little cut on my hand but I've fixed it up."

"Don't ever try and walk home in a Taku wind again," I warned. "Get a cab."

"I know now what a Taku wind is like," she commented dryly.

The winter passed swiftly. Fern went home to Kennewick just before Christmas. I missed her but was too busy to be lonely for long. With shorter days and gloomier weather I also found I could easily spend more time sleeping. I walked a lot but seldom went out in the country.

During a cold spell the temperature dropped near zero and the ice froze thick enough for skating on Auke Lake, twelve miles from town. I found time to ride the bus out with friends several days before the weather moderated and a foot of snow put an end to the skating.

After coming home from work at midnight, I often stood outside and watched the lights of Juneau, from the A.J. mill, seeing clearly boarding houses clinging to the steep mountainside, right down to the harbor lights outlining the channel. A stream of tiny lights from the miners acetylene headlamps, winding down the trail at the end of a shift fascinated me. Sometimes I could make out the forms of ships berthed at the wharf.

"Some day I'm going to be on one of those ships headed even farther north," I promised myself. Seward, Fairbanks, Kotzebue, Chilkoot Pass, all names I had read about, appealed to me.

2

To the "Westward"

The gnawing knowledge that there was still a lot of Alaska to the "Westward" that I knew nothing of and the independence born of money in the bank, prompted me to sell my interest in the café business. I had wearied of the long hours and when I almost dreaded seeing customers come through the door, I decided it was time for a change. I withdrew $500 from my savings and spent better than fifty dollars for passage on the SS McKinley. This time there would not be the urgency to find work when I got to where I was going.

On my last day in Juneau I received a letter from my mother, saying she hoped I wouldn't go any farther north. I had a fleeting moment of indecisiveness and guilt but my mind was made up and my ticket was in my pocket.

This was my first trip on a big steamship, and with its dining tables under snowy white coverings, rows of shiny silverware, elaborate menus and stateroom service at the ring of a bell, it was pure luxury. During the three-day crossing of the Gulf of Alaska I had ample time to investigate each deck and relax in the lounge or observation room. Although much of the time there was nothing to see but the ocean in every direction, I walked outside several times a day to enjoy the cool crisp air. It was considered a smooth crossing, however I felt a mild effect from the long swells, but luckily not enough for me to miss any meals.

An air of anticipation and expectancy pervaded the ship. Alaska residents were eagerly looking forward to being home again after weeks or months Outside. Others were anxious to return for summer employment in the mines, fishing or other types of work. Those who were first-timers displayed much

16

curiosity about every phase of the journey as well as the ship, the people, the country and scenery. The look on their faces and their questions revealed anxiety and uncertainty, feelings with which I was familiar. There were a few native Indians and Eskimos who mingled freely with passengers to whom they were obviously acquainted. Everyone was so friendly I didn't feel alone or uncomfortable for long. Many of the old-timers, perhaps bored after many such trips, seemed willing, indeed welcomed, the opportunity to talk to newcomers, answering questions, advising or sharing experiences and sometimes regaling a wide-eyed listener with a farfetched story.

In the darkness of early morning, the *McKinley* docked in Seward, a small but busy seaport in Resurrection Bay and the end of the line for regularly scheduled runs by passenger ships of the Alaska Steamship Company. Eagerly I peeked out the porthole at the lights of the city and the longshoremen who were gathering to start unloading the freight. When I went on deck at daylight I thought I had never seen any setting so beautiful as the picturesque circular harbor against a background of rugged snowcovered mountains glistening in the early sun. I was nearly 600 miles farther north and a long ways from any friends.

Seward was the southern terminus of the Alaska Railroad. The end of the line was nearly 500 miles north. I was going further on so I went directly to the train waiting at the nearby station. The train passed through densely wooded country, then along Turnagain Arm to Anchorage, at that time a city of nearly 4000, located near the head of Cook Inlet. After sharing a cab with a fellow-traveler I checked in at the Anchorage Hotel. The lobby was crowded with people; packsacks and luggage were piled in every available space.

"May I have the key to my room?" I asked the lady clerk after her husband had picked up my suitcases and started for the stairs.

"We don't have any keys," she said smiling. "You don't need one here, dear," she assured me. I harbored no qualms, so willing was I to fit into all aspects of life in the north. I had already learned, after a year in Alaska, that I need have little fear of robberies. Hadn't I walked home night after night from the café in Juneau, carrying the day's proceeds in a money bag, making no attempt to conceal it? I had always wondered if the one big deterrent to crime was the limited means of leaving the country. We had heard that occasionally a law-breaker would be met by the police as he came down the gangplank in Seattle. Air service

17

to Alaska was just starting. Trial runs were under way with the Pan American Clipper, or Flying Boat, and later land-based planes would be used.

There was still about a foot of snow on the ground in Anchorage so I confined my walking during my explorations to the wide streets of the city, which were well laid out near the banks of Cook Inlet. I did follow a road, which was just beginning to thaw, to the airport where bush pilots were busy loading their small planes with packsacks, groceries, mail and parts of machinery for flights to small villages or mines out in the bush.

I was glad to see Helen Harper again. She had indeed homesteaded a tract of land and when not there lived in an apartment while working in a laundry. On weekends she would hike six miles to work on her cabin alone. Starry-eyed, she told me that now she had met a man. The new emotions that lighted up her face as she spoke of him were becoming and as I looked at her I wondered if I might also meet someone that would fit into my plans.

I liked Anchorage and could easily have stayed there but I had started for Fairbanks and was determined to go on to see the midnight sun. So I boarded the train again, one of perhaps seventy or eighty passengers, and found one vacant seat in the car I was directed to. "Mind if I share the seat with you, young lady?" a neatly dressed man of about sixty asked as I settled down next to the window.

"Not at all," I answered, "but I might pester you with endless questions."

"And you've just answered my next question," he said, smiling. "This must be your first trip on the train." He was of medium stature and had pleasant features.

"My name is McPherson but everyone calls me Mac," he offered this information while removing his hat and heavy coat. "I work a small gold mine fifty miles out of Fairbanks," he went on, getting comfortable. "Those four young fellows across the aisle work with me, they're college boys." He then explained that he and his wife had lived in Alaska for twenty-five years but now had a home in Seattle. His wife could not stand the mosquitoes at the mining camp, so she stayed in Seattle where their youngest daughter also lived.

As we went along, Mac pointed out a homesteader's cabin beside a creek and another one alongside a thicket of bare birch trees. Twice the train whistled, and each time an adult moose trotted away from the tracks. Brief stops were made at small settlements where a few people with dogs would gather to watch the arrival of the train. Going through the Palmer area, a light covering of snow could not hide the evidence of farmed land, and then as the train glided through mile after mile of mountainous country and dense spruce forests, I began to wonder if there was going to be no end to this wilderness. Had I come too far this time?

"Now what brings you to Alaska?" Mac finally asked me, after I had been questioning him for at least an hour.

"I guess I just always wanted to go north," I replied, then told him some of the events of the past year.

"You have spunk," he said. "You'll make a good Alaskan."

Miles later my curiosity was aroused again.

"I don't think it's strange that *I* came to Alaska," I confided, "but I can't help wondering what brought these other people north."

"Alaska is a hodgepodge of humanity," he answered musingly. "Some, like you, come for adventure. I came up as a young mining engineer and stayed on to mine for myself. A lot come for summer work. Others, like those," glancing toward a young couple with two children, "might be looking for new frontiers and a more independent way of life. Some are dreamers and they'll give up when the going gets tough. And then there are those who hope to make a quick fortune by whatever means available."

Mac sat quietly for a full minute before continuing.

"You know, I really believe there's a lot of people come up here to try to escape something, a messed up marriage maybe, disappointments, responsibilities or plain boredom. Others are just drifters."

It was still daylight when the train pulled into Curry for the overnight stop at a large hotel, the only hotel in the small settlement. Both the hotel and the railroad were operated by the government so there was no choice for passengers but to take rooms there and eat in the spacious dining room. I was invited to have dinner with Mac and his boys and was amazed at the various choices on the menu, attractively served on white tablecloths by uniformed waiters. I was tired so went to my room shortly after dinner and fell asleep immediately.

After a satisfying breakfast of ham and eggs the next morning, we boarded the train again and continued north. It appeared to be a promising day; only a few light clouds hovered over the mountains. It wasn't long before the conductor announced that there would soon be a view of Mt. McKinley. He

19

remarked we might be fortunate enough to see the whole mountain as clouds often hung over the top and on some days no part of it was visible at all. I was totally unprepared for the sight of that gigantic snow-covered mass, glowing radiantly against the now cloudless sky. It dwarfed all else in sight. Even at a distance of possibly fifty miles, it seemed to loom directly over us. Mt. McKinley's 20,300 foot (6,187 metres) height rises from a level of 2000 feet (609 metres); in comparison, Mt. Whitney begins at a level of 8000 feet (2,440 metres), its total height being only 14,500 (4,420 metres).

Sometime after passing through Healy, a small coalmining town, the landscape changed to sparse scrubby trees and miles of muskeg dotted with strange-looking hummocks of earth, supposedly caused by extreme freezing conditions. We crossed the still frozen Tanana River at Nenana, where the ice-breakup takes place each year, and by early afternoon the train whistled its arrival at the depot in Fairbanks.

"This is it!" I said to myself as I stepped off of the train. "I made it, I'm in Fairbanks!"

I checked into a room at the Northern Hotel for three dollars a day, then went out to see the sights. This city of nearly 3000, divided by the Chena River, was a mixture of new and old buildings and log cabins. The ground was beginning to thaw and the unpaved streets were muddy.

"Want to go across?" a husky bewhiskered fellow nearby asked me as I stood on a corner wondering if my galoshes were adequate to wade through the mud. Before I could answer he picked me up and carried me across the street. As I was stammering a 'thank you', I saw two little girls standing nearby giggling. They nodded their heads when my rescuer approached them with the same question and were still giggling as he started across the street with one tucked under each arm.

Almost before I wanted to, I saw a 'help wanted' sign in the window of the Tivoli Cafe and was hired on the spot when I inquired. It was the largest restaurant in town, having a counter with twenty stools along its length, and a fountain, as well as a long row of booths which could be enclosed by curtains. I would learn later that a discreetly drawn curtain usually meant that a lady from the red-light district was being wined and dined by an admirer.

I had never worked in a large professionally operated restaurant before. As a result I experienced some hectic times and was often impatiently reprimanded by the Greek cooks before I learned to call in orders and serve a three or four course dinner properly. We did not turn in written meal orders, but called them in, and woe be it if we blundered. The cooks prided themselves on the number of orders they could remember in sequence so it was imperative to itemize briefly and accurately. We wore black uniforms with little white aprons and waited on all who came in, dirty unshaven men in rough attire, right alongside people in evening clothes.

I was surprised at the elaborate menus with a choice of many entrees, from roast turkey to fried cornmeal mush, considering that everything had to be shipped in by steamship and railroad. Obviously eating out was a favorite pastime in Fairbanks, and since the men outnumbered the women five to one, restaurants were kept busy.

Although the cooks were quite steady, there was a big turnover among the waitresses. Most were wives wanting temporary work, or girls waiting for something better to come along, and some, like myself, were more or less experienced and willing to work.

One day I overheard one of the cooks, a fiery-tempered little fellow, complain about my inexperience to an elderly dishwasher.

"Give her time, give her time," the older Greek remonstrated.

Later I was to gloat with satisfaction over the little fellow's look of approval when time after time I was the only, or at least only sober waitress to show up for work on a busy morning shift.

"See, I tell you," I heard the old fellow remind the little Greek cook.

"I fix you something," one of them would say when I had time to eat. Often it was a choice steak or other bits of tasty food. In all fairness I must say there were other dependable girls, but most of them preferred the afternoon or evening shifts.

Shortly after arriving in Fairbanks I learned that an old friend of my mother's, Mrs. Finley, who was a widow, was living in the city with her son and family. She was as pleased as I when we arranged to live together in a rented log cabin with two large rooms and an enclosed back porch. It was conveniently located for both of us, only six blocks from the main downtown street. Mrs. Finley sold Avon products and worked at babysitting.

"I'll get the honey-man coming right away," she told me the day we moved in.

"Honey-man?" I exclaimed, puzzled.

She laughed at my surprise then explained. "You know there is no sewer system here. The winters are too cold, pipes would freeze, the ground never thaws more than a couple feet deep."

"But what do the hotels and business places do?" I asked.

"The business district and some of the modern homes have their own arrangement of some kind of steam heated pipes, I believe," she answered.

Privately owned trucks came by regularly and changed the five gallon cans. The small coal-oil heater made it tolerable inside the privy but we stepped quickly when passing over the unheated porch.

The days lengthened rapidly until by June there was no darkness at all. The sun would go out of sight below the horizon briefly, but never long enough to lose its glow. I felt the lack of sleep before I became accustomed to twenty-four hours of daylight. It was hard to live by the clock with the temptation to continue work or play because it still seemed like daytime.

"Let's go to the baseball game at midnight," Mrs. Finley proposed after I had finished my shift on the longest day of the year.

"A ball game at midnight?" I exclaimed.

"Sure, they play every year at midnight on the twenty-first, and without lights," she said.

It was a lively game supported by a wildly enthusiastic audience. Liquor was much in evidence resulting in a few minor fights. In spite of the noisy merrymaking, firecrackers and daylight, I could hardly stay awake until four o'clock when Mrs. Finley and I left for home. The celebration was still going strong.

I had little free time to get interested in romance, often working overtime or filling in on other shifts. However, I had kept a wary eye open but it appeared to me that all the men seemed to be married, were too old, were working out on the creeks or mostly hung around the saloons. I was more dis-appointed because I didn't have much time to explore the surrounding country, but I was content just to be there — to be involved in the daily life of this bustling old gold-rush town. A waitress friend and I did find time to visit the museum, explore the city itself and walk along some of the dusty roads where we discovered bright orange columbine, the purple bells of foxglove, the red splash of wild geraniums and the fragrant wild roses.

"Listen!" I suddenly exclaimed as we walked along the river bank one evening. I stopped and looked up towards the sky.

"What is it?" my friend asked. The honking sounds were unmistakable.

"It's Canada geese," I said. "See, there!" There were only a few of the big birds flying quite low and they soon disappeared.

"It must be a local bunch that stay along the river," I said.

22

Then I confided to her that I remembered as a youngster standing watching a big V-shaped flock of wild geese flying so high in the sky, I could just barely hear their steady outcry. I was curious to know where they were going and why they flew so steadily to the north. What strange lands did they seek beyond the horizon? Beyond my little world? I was envious of their freedom to go wherever it was they were going while I remained earthbound in a weedy potato patch.

My companion smiled then said seriously, "You've come a long way since then."

The dry sunny days were a welcome change from the excessive rains of Juneau. I was surprised to see the temperature had reached 100 degrees one day; it didn't seem that warm. Usually it was moderately warm; short refreshing showers were frequent with an occasional electric storm. Flower gardens bloomed profusely. Bright showy nasturtiums blossomed in abundance until the frosts came; the leaves of some growing to measure six inches across.

The days and weeks passed swiftly. Due to the unsettling war conditions in Europe, construction had begun on Ladd Air Force Base at Fairbanks. Every train brought more workers and the restaurant became increasingly busy. The first of September I took a weeks' vacation and left on a trip to the village of Circle on the Yukon River, 150 miles northeast of Fairbanks. I shared expenses with a young doctor and his wife, Tom and Muriel. We traveled in their car on a narrow dirt road that wound through scrub brush and bright yellow tamarack trees, and over rolling hills. Ptarmigan, a northern grouse, dusting themselves on the road, would not move until the car was almost upon them.

It was a beautiful sunny day but there were signs of recent frost, which had at least put an end to the mosquitoes, but it also warned that the short summer was already yielding to more harsh forces coming from the Arctic. The precious daylight hours were lessening day by day. We watched for migrating caribou herds but failed to see any.

Late in the afternoon we arrived at Circle Hot Springs, a tiny community about twenty-five miles from Circle. The lodge where we stayed was heated by the water from the hot springs and we found the hot baths most relaxing after the dusty drive. I saw an unbelievably lush garden which was also heated by piping the hot water through it. All the vegetation adjoining the heated portion was frozen down flat.

The next day we drove to Circle and I finally stood on the bank of the famous Yukon River. I was elated! I had reached the

23

end of the road and was on the fringe of the Arctic Circle. I tried to appear calm, to hide the exhilaration and sense of satisfaction I felt inside but knew I had failed when I saw the doctor watching me curiously.

"How long have you looked forward to this?" he asked.

"Forever, I believe," I replied.

"Let's go see where that fishy smell comes from," Muriel interrupted.

We walked down the river a short distance to where Indians were unloading twenty or thirty salmon from a long riverboat pulled up on the sandy shore. Other natives butchered, split and cut the fish in wide strips and hung them over racks six or eight feet high. In answer to our questions, they told us the sun would get warm enough today to start drying the fish, but that before evening they would build a small fire under the rack.

"How do they keep the flies off?" I asked later.

"The frost has slowed them down now," Dr. Tom answered, "usually they're thick, along with the yellow jackets, which make the Indians happy because the bees eat the flies, eggs and the maggots."

Children and dogs played along the dusty road and around a scattering of small unpainted houses surrounded by broken-down toys, boat motors and other litter. We stopped at a larger square-built log structure which bore the name "Northern Commercial Company" over the door. Referred to as the N.C., similar to the Hudson's Bay Company, it was Alaska's major trading firm, often the only store in the smaller villages.

While Tom and Muriel spoke with the storekeeper, a white man, I looked at the fascinating conglomeration of goods. The shelves were stacked with groceries that included powdered milk, hard tack, canned butter and bacon, as well as corn flakes and ginger snaps. On one side of the big room hung long underwear, prominently displayed over fish lines strung between pegs. Wool jackets and shirts, fur-lined parkas, mukluks, rubber pacs, snowshoes and other clothing were stacked along the wall. Steel traps of various sizes, fishing gear, nets, tools and various hardware hung on another wall. A huge pot-bellied stove dominated the center of the room. No doubt it would be a much sought after gathering place after the snows came.

While I watched, two women came in bringing mukluks to trade for groceries. The tops of the boots were made of some sort of fur and the soles and lower part were no doubt shaped from caribou hide. The storekeeper seemed to have no trouble understanding their throaty thick manner of speech, and they soon went away; everyone concerned seeming to be happy with the bargaining.

After two more days of relaxation at the Hot Springs Lodge and what proved to be an unfruitful attempt at panning gold, I bought several small nuggets from an old bearded prospector. His handmade "poke", a small rawhide bag, was half full of gold, from tiny flakes to nuggets the size of small marbles. His answer was evasive when I asked him if that was this summer's gleaning. Gold was then worth not more than twenty dollars an ounce.

We had traveled nearly fifty miles on the return trip, when Muriel suddenly exclaimed, "Look there!"

"It looks like the whole hillside is moving!" I added in amazement. Dr. Tom stopped the car and we scrambled out.

"It's caribou, they're migrating south," he said. While we stood wide-eyed, less than a half mile away the dark mass poured over the brow of a low hill and spread down the slope. A forest of antlers gleamed sporadically in the sun; lighter spots on the dark hides blended in with the landscape.

We watched until the last stragglers trotted out of sight.

"This tops off an already great vacation," I said with a happy sigh.

Back in Fairbanks, October finally brought snow flurries and a steady decline in temperatures. Every day bush pilots brought in workers from the mines and the 'creeks', which referred to mines usually situated along waterways. Old-timers with huge nuggets dangling from watchchains mingled with new construction workers glad to be back to civilization after a summer in the mosquito-infested bush. The restaurant fairly vibrated with their exuberance, some excited to be going Outside and others celebrating a prosperous season. Tips were generous. Saloons were crowded and noisy with their juke boxes blaring continuously. More and more often the curtains were drawn around the booths at the Tivoli Cafe.

Inevitably there was also some heartbreak and disappointment. I wondered about the moody men who sat quietly at the counter drinking endless cups of coffee. What troubled them? Who or what were they trying to escape? With the tongue-loosening effect of a couple of drinks, a few would share their problems with anyone who would listen. Some vented their frustrations on others or tried to drink their troubles away.

"Don't you feel well?" I asked one day of a teary-eyed waitress who never missed a shift. She and I had become good friends.

"My husband gambled away his paycheck last night," she

replied with quivering lips. I touched her arm briefly; I dared not risk shattering her brave attempt at composure by showing more sympathy. Customers needed to be waited on.

"I'll take part of your section today," I assured her as we both tied on our aprons.

One day the irate husband of one of the waitresses stalked into the restaurant, well-fortified from the bottle conspicuous in his hip pocket. Not so conspicuous was the butt end of a gun protruding from his coat pocket. The cook, who was under suspicion of being involved with the waitress, locked himself in the toilet and stayed there long after friends had persuaded the jealous man to leave.

I heard a few people, usually women who were not there by choice, complain bitterly about the isolation, the loneliness, the inconveniences and rough-cut character of the old gold towns. And yet, while walking home one day, a taxi pulled up to the curb ahead of me and several people in long white dresses and tuxedos came out of an old log house to be whisked away. Farther on I paused a moment in front of a church to listen to the soothing music of an organ.

I now worked an evening shift at the fountain, a welcome change which I had requested. Every night I made from twenty-five to forty gallons of ice cream. The liquid mix sealed in five-gallon cans was shipped in by boat and rail. I added the various flavors as needed. The amount of ice cream consumed during the wintertime was unbelievable; it went by cones, dishes, quarts or even a gallon for some party. Beside the usual popular flavors, every week I made a few gallons of some special flavor such as peppermint, pumpkin or berry.

Aline Harwick, a friend from Juneau who now lived in Fairbanks with her husband, often went for short walks with me during the brief daylight hours. We would skirt the edge of the town, sometimes passing a fenced-in yard full of snarling malamutes or huskies, renowned for their use as sled dogs. When some of them lunged against the fence, the hair on their necks bristling, we quickened our pace. Then, instead of having a cup of coffee, as would seem logical after a walk in twenty below zero temperatures, we stopped at the fountain for a milkshake. There's something about cold air devoid of moisture, that makes one dry and thirsty. Years later I read an article in a newspaper stating that Fairbanks consumed more ice cream per capita than any other city in the United States.

As winter progressed, I continued to walk to and from work in temperatures that fluctuated around twenty below. When colder or stormy I would call a cab. By now most private cars were bedded down for the winter and cab drivers had to keep their motors running continually. The shrill squeal of tires on hard packed snow could be heard for several blocks.

"I'm going home for Christmas," I announced one evening in early December as Mrs. Finley and I walked home together from a movie. She was quiet a few moments. I wondered if maybe she felt an urge to go south too. Lights glimmered behind drawn shades in houses we passed. Our clumsy boots squeaked on the frozen snow.

"I'm going to miss you," my companion finally replied, "but I know your mother will be happy to see you."

"But I'll be back," I hastened to assure her as well as myself. "I really do like it here."

It had been nearly two years since I came north and I was wearying of the long hours at the cafe, work that didn't especially appeal to me but had served its purpose well.

Now it started to snow, drifting down lazily; snow so dry and fine it accumulated slowly. There was less than a foot on the ground. A dog howled in the distance; another in the opposite direction seemed to answer. Still another joined in until a spine-tingling chorus encircled the city.

"Sounds like wolves," I said, shivering.

"It's malamutes and huskies," Mrs. Finley explained. "Malamutes are supposedly part-wolf, at least several generations back, and many are vicious. City law says all dogs have to be either penned in or tied up."

Long after I had gone to bed I still heard the mournful, yearning howls. I wondered whether the creatures were frustrated at the chains that held them captive from the silent beckoning of their wilderness heritage?

The midnight walks home from work were unforgettable. The sight of the tiny cluster of city lights enfolded in a vast sea of darkness gave the illusion of an infinitesimal island on top of the world. At times the solitude of empty streets and glimmering stars was soothing after a hectic day. Other times, I felt the exhilaration of leaning into the biting snow, well protected by wool mitts and scarves.

Often I stood spellbound by the swaying streamers of the Northern Lights (Aurora Borealis), shimmering green interspersed with white streaks. They were like beams from a giant spotlight moving slowly across the heavens. Other times a rosy glow serpentined from horizon to horizon. Only when I began to feel the penetrating cold did I move on to the warmth of the coal burning stove in our cozy home.

On the morning of December 12 I bade Mrs. Finley goodbye.

"I'll wait for you if you would like to go south with me," I offered. I knew she longed to see sons and grandchildren in Washington state.

"No," she answered composed and smiling. "I'll stay and look for that old man with a poke full of gold and a bad cough."

It was dark and twenty-six below zero when I boarded the train to Seward. Only briefly during the dusky light of midday did I have glimpses of the white world we passed through. There was no sign of life. It was as if the vast wilderness had stopped breathing.

If I had known what the trip across the Gulf of Alaska could be like in the middle of winter, I would never have gone at that time. For four days and nights I lay in my bunk, unable to eat a bite, while the steamer *Yukon*, pitched and rolled. One minute I would see the hazy sky through the porthole and the next moment I was looking at green violent water. By the third day my insides ached from my continual retching. My only relief was when I lay perfectly still. Several years later this same steamship broke in half during a fierce storm. The forward section, with survivors, went aground on a reef.

A few minutes after we entered the quiet waters of the inland passage I was able to get up, dress and eat a good meal. As the *Yukon* cruised southward I luxuriated in the comfort of the large vessel but it was the trip north on the little *Tongass* that would always remain more vivid in my memories. Even as I stepped off the gang-plank in Seattle I glanced back and whispered, "I'll be back."

3

Honeymoon A-Fishing

"Here's mail for you from Alaska," my mother said, looking over a handful of letters and papers she had just brought in from the country mailbox alongside a road near our house. I sat in the front room and eagerly opened two letters from friends, then devoured every bit of news in a Juneau newspaper. For a long time I sat quietly before I walked slowly to the kitchen and hugged my mother.

"I'm sorry, Mom ," I started to explain.

"I know, you're going back. It's all right." She blinked to hide a tear. I knew she longed for her children to settle somewhere near but never did she attempt to discourage either Fern or myself to go north. I had enjoyed mingling with my family and former school friends again and had honestly considered the possibility of finding work and being content to stay. But I soon realized I was hopelessly addicted to Alaska, the country the Aleut Indians had named "The Great Land." I watched the papers and listened to the radio for every bit of news possible about the northland. I watched for the flight north of the Canada geese and stood outside at night looking to the sky and wondering if the Northern Lights were on display up north.

"Where will you go this time?" my mother asked, quickly regaining her composure.

"I'm not sure, but I'll go to Juneau first," I replied. "I want to see friends there and stay with Fern a while." Fern had returned to Juneau while I was in Fairbanks and now had a steady boyfriend.

"Yes, I'm glad you'll see her," Mom said. "I'll only have to write half as many letters then."

29

Two weeks later I was again in Juneau, happy to see Fern and friends, to walk familiar streets, to breathe deeply of the piquant scent of the lush evergreens mixed with the salty seabreeze.

"It's just the same as it was the first day we set foot here," I observed as Fern and I walked along the waterfront on a rainy day.

"Except we're not as scared as we were then," Fern said. "And there's plenty to eat this time. Let's go and fry a big slice of fresh salmon for dinner."

Within a few days an acquaintance asked me to help out in her small dress shop while her regular clerk was off indefinitely because of illness in her family. That suited me because I didn't want to commit myself to anything steady yet but felt content to stay in Juneau for the time being.

My eight-hour job gave me more time for recreation. I joined a bowling team, went to church, rode the bus out into the country and was often invited to the Scandinavian dances, which I really enjoyed. Due to the predominantly male population women did not lack for dates, but I shied away from any which involved entertainment at the bars or night clubs, both popular pastimes. I was fortunate to have a few friends who owned small boats and was often invited out for a ride.

"Do you like your work at the dress shop?" a friend, Lucille Johnson asked one day when we met at the post office.

"Oh, it's alright," I answered, "but it's temporary. I'll stay until I decide to go north."

"There's an opening in the bookkeeping department at B.M. Behrends Bank where I work," Lucille said. "Why don't you try for it? I think you would do well there and you can always go north later. There's lots of time for that."

"I've never really done that kind of work," I said a bit dubiously, "but I have always been good with mathematics."

"I know you can do it and I can help you," Lucille encouraged. "You'll like the people working there, too. Why don't you go over and talk to Mr. Mullen. He's the president."

I was tempted. I liked working with figures and the idea of being involved with the workings of a bank was intriguing. It would give me an opportunity to save more money to continue my travels in Alaska without the need of going to work right away.

"Come to work Monday morning at eight o'clock," Mr. Mullen said after a less than five minute interview. There were no questions concerning references or qualifications. Pleased with the new type of work and new associates, I became aware of a small measure of the prestige attributed to the banking business. My beginning pay was $110 a month, much less than I had realized at the bus depot cafe two years earlier, but I was satisfied. After all, I confided to myself, this is pretty good for a farm girl and apple-packer from Kennewick.

Fern had married and I now paid thirty dollars a month for a comfortable two-room apartment with bath and a large closet and a good view of the town and harbor from its location on one of the hilly streets. In the winter it required some agile footwork to stay upright when the streets and boardwalks were coated with ice and snow. There were cleats on some of the steeper sidewalks as a safety measure because the abundance of rain kept them slippery much of the time.

While eating breakfast on the wintry morning of December 7th, 1941, I heard of the bombing of Pearl Harbor over the local radio station. Later in the day I went skating on Auke Lake with friends. Although the usual cheerfulness and banter among the skaters was much subdued, I did not realize myself the full impact of the war until the city was blacked out. Many changes took place in the next few weeks. Young men left to enter the service, navy boats showed up in the harbor, army camps were set up in the country and many new faces appeared on the streets. The city seemed feverish with military activities.

On the cold New Year's Eve of 1942 I met Stewart Neely at a mutual friend's home. A quiet stalwart man with keen blue eyes and dark hair, I thought him decidedly good-looking. As he walked me home in the early hours of the new year, each step crunched and squeaked on the frosty snow. The dark form of Mt. Roberts loomed large over the lights of Juneau nestled at its foot.

"I sure like him but what's the use, he's going south tomorrow and I'll never see him again," I was thinking.

"Will you have dinner with me tomorrow?" he asked at the door of my apartment.

"But I thought you had reserved passage on the *Aleutian* tomorrow," I stammered.

"I did," he answered softly, "but I've decided to cancel it. How about the dinner?"

The following evening we lingered over coffee in the dining room of the Baranof Hotel. Stewart spoke of his folks living in Auburn, Washington, descendants of pioneers who settled in that area. His great grandfather was a lieutenant at the Blockhouse in Seattle during some of the Indian Wars.

"When did you first come to Alaska?" I asked.

31

"I was eighteen when I got a summer's job with Libby, McNeill and Libby as one of the cannery crew going to Nushagak, Alaska," he told me. "We sailed on the *Admiral W.W. Gorgas*, a coal-burning German ship, captured during World War I and purchased by Libby's to be used as a cannery ship north to the Bering Sea."

He explained that the ship had carried a crew of Filipinos who worked ashore in the salmon cannery. He had been one of the crew that worked on a scow anchored offshore, where the fishermen unloaded their catches. It was dangerous work in the frequently stormy weather. The fishing fleet owned by the company was all sailboats; mechanical power in Bristol Bay was prohibited by law. The crewmen were paid a percentage of the season's proceeds.

It happened to be a poor fishing season so Stu's share for three months work was disappointing and considerably below normal even in 1927.

"I went home with three 100 dollar bills," he concluded. "I kept them for a while and kids from all over town came to our house to see a $100 bill."

Several years later he had come to Juneau to fish commercially. For some time before Pearl Harbor he had worked at the naval base in Sitka and now he was on his way to visit his folks before entering the service.

In the weeks that followed there were many such dinners together at the city's three most popular restaurants. Several times when the weather was agreeable we hiked the two and a half miles to have dinner with my sister and her husband, George Troychak. They lived in a rented house overlooking Gastineau Channel and George worked for the Bureau of Public Roads. Sometimes Stu came up the hill to my apartment with a package containing two steaks and we had a quiet evening with music, if it came in, over the radio.

All too swiftly a month passed and my new friend resumed his delayed trip south. Now I had a new interest in the steamships that came from the south rather than those going north. As each one came in I wondered if there would be a letter on it and hurried to the post office after work. My traveling plans had taken a new direction and for the first time, Alaska was not uppermost in my thoughts.

I continued working at the bank for six months, then after increasingly persuasive letters and the realization of the uncertainty of wartime plans, I went south and fifteen months after we first met, Stewart and I were making plans to be married on one of his weekend leaves from Fort Lewis. At the last moment he was unexpectedly transferred to Camp Abbott in Oregon. Two weeks later he was sent to the army hospital in Walla Walla, Washington for medical attention. Learning there would be two or three weeks' wait for corrective surgery, he made an appointment with the chaplain and called me, only to have a routine dental appointment take priority over the wedding.

Two days later, on May 11, 1944, Stu was issued a few days leave and we hurried to a justice of peace, not taking any more chances with the army's unpredictable whims.

"Looks like we finally made it," I whispered as a girl led us into a room where a grayhaired man with a kindly face and friendly manner greeted us with a warm handshake.

A few questions about ourselves led to a sociable exchange between the judge and Stewart regarding mutual outdoor interests. Inevitably the talk turned to fishing while I stood there impatiently shifting from one foot to the other, wondering if they had both forgotten why we were there. Finally the judge called in two secretaries for witnesses and the brief ceremony was over in much less time than was spent on fishing talk.

After being discharged from the hospital, my husband was given a thirty-day convalescent furlough. We loaded our Ford roadster at his folks' home in Auburn, and with a few carefully hoarded gas stamps we were ready to leave for Vancouver Island in Canada.

"It's within reach of our gas supply," Stu said, "and I've heard the fishing is good up there, too." It was the first hint I had that this would be a fishing honeymoon but not having known anything about the ways of avid fishermen, I had no qualms. Like Helen Harper, I was happy with the man I married regardless of where he chose to go.

"Virginia, are you sure this is what you want to do?" my mother-in-law ventured hesitantly, as she watched her son pack the fishing poles in the car. "A fishing trip on your honeymoon?" I assured her I loved fishing although I had only gone fishing once with Stu, the first time ever for me.

In spite of anxiety over wartime conditions and the uncertainty of what might happen after Stu's furlough ended, we were happy and excited as we drove to Anacortes to board the ferry for Sydney. I remember the fields of white daisies as we drove north on the island on a bright sunny day, and the neat homes with attractive yards of colorful flowers. Stu kept watching for a good place to wet a fish line along the waterfront of the small towns.

The next day about noon we drove into Courtenay. After making a few inquiries at the cafe where we ate lunch we learned that a few salmon were being caught around Comox, a small town four or five miles distant. We were also directed to a hotel several blocks away.

To our surprise the hotel was a very large English style building, old but pretentious, the surrounding grounds beautifully landscaped. As soon as we stepped inside and I felt a thick carpet under my feet I knew we were in the wrong place. Not about to be intimidated by a plush carpet, my husband strode right up to the desk where a gentleman in English tweeds and necktie took one look at us over the top of his specs and said, "Sorry, there are no rooms available."

Stu was unperturbed by the obvious rebuff because of our comfortable but plain and undoubtedly rumpled traveling clothes. I only wanted to get out of there. We drove on down to the waterfront at Comox, parked the car and walked out on the dock.

"Anyone catching salmon here?" Stu asked a friendly group of men idling nearby.

"There's a few here but they're not easy to catch," was the response. "You need a big brass flasher and a white plug. And they only bite early in the morning and in the evening."

"Does anyone ever use herring for bait?" Stu asked.

"Oh no, the salmon won't bite on herring," was the answer.

As we walked on to the end of the dock, I gazed around at the sights but my husband intently watched the water. Suddenly he exclaimed, "Just look at those herring!" The water darkened as a school of herring swirled and flipped. Soon a silvery streak broke water scattering the herring in all directions.

"Did you see that? It was a salmon chasing herring!" Stu burst out.

That was all he needed. In a few minutes he had his pole out and we were down on one of the floats the fishing boats were tied to. First of all he easily caught some herring. Carefully putting a strip cut from the herring on the hook, he raised his rod and cast out thirty or forty feet, stripping in slowly to get the proper action on the spinner. "Is that what you call strip fishing?" I questioned as he cast out again and repeated the maneuver.

"That's right," he nodded. At this time there were no casting reels and fishing lines were made of (cat) gut. By stripping his line into a basket or onto the floor-boards of the boat a fisherman could then cast it out with his rod and a flick of the wrist. Nylon lines were just beginning to be used and we bought our first in

Canada.

A cut spinner working properly resembles a crippled herring and it wasn't long before a gullible salmon was after it. The pole bent in an arc!

"You've got one! You've got one!" I shouted.

Stu heaved back on it to set the hook, the reel started whirring—music to a fisherman's ears—and the fight was on! After several fast runs the salmon tired and was in close to the float when we realized the landing net was still in the car. A fisherman who had been watching from his trolling boat nearby offered his gaff hook and Stu soon landed a nice thirty-two pound king. Within the hour he- caught two more good sized ones.

By this time several people had gathered to watch. They had never seen this method of fishing before; a limber pole, ten-pound test line and cut herring for bait.

"Anyone know where I can rent a row boat?" Stu asked. Forgotten was the need to find lodging.

"You're welcome to use mine in exchange for a salmon or two," an elderly man offered.

"What are you aiming to do with your salmon?" the man on the trolling boat inquired. "You know it's wartime," he went on, "we need the food. I'll buy all you can't use."

As nonresidents we couldn't legally sell fish but were easily convinced that it would be supporting the war effort. Then he asked where we were staying and when we told him we were looking for lodging, he mentioned that although he lived in Courtenay he would be staying on his boat most of the summer. His wife would be alone and he thought she would be glad to rent us a spare room.

"Just go up and tell her I sent you," he said. We did, and she accepted us without question, offering us the use of the kitchen as well. By evening we were moved in and well pleased with the events of the day. We had a boat to use, a market for any surplus salmon and a pleasant place to live. Already we liked Canada. The Farleys were lovely people and before we left we became good friends.

The fishing was better than we ever hoped for due to the abundant herring feeding in the bay. We knew when they left, the salmon would also leave, so there was no question what our activity for the day would be.

"Here, let me show you again," Stu said a dozen times a day as I tried repeatedly to cut a spinner properly. But it was two weeks before I managed to do one that was considered acceptable. So far I had found Stu to be an easy going person, not at all fussy or a stickler for perfection, but it didn't take long for me to learn that he didn't tolerate sloppy bait-cutting, dull fish hooks, frayed lines or clumsy knots. Striving for a 'well-done' from this avid fisherman, I soon became quite adept at casting, stripping and playing the elusive salmon. But at times when I was tired, my hair a mess, everything smelled of fish and I found herring scales stuck to my hands at the dinner table, I had second thoughts about spending a honeymoon on a fishing trip.

Stu's method of fishing was creating considerable interest in the vicinity and he willingly shared his know-how and secrets.

"I'm using a light-weight line so the salmon can't see it," he explained. "Then you can catch them in daytime as well as morning and evening."

He demonstrated how a light limber pole yields more easily to the jerks and tugs of a fighting fish than a heavy rigid one, consequently shifting the pull to the reel and allowing for a smooth flow of line. Every day he showed someone how to jig for herring, cut spinners and bait hooks. Such generosity isn't at all typical of a fisherman, but these people were so friendly and accommodating that even a hard-core angler couldn't resist sharing.

Day after day we reveled in the sunshine and good fishing. traffic in the bay from a British Navy training base, less than two miles from the Comox docks, reminded us that we were still involved in a war. One day we were fishing from our borrowed skiff which was tied to one of the pilings. Herring were milling around and under the dock, feeding and followed by the gluttonous salmon. A navy barge glided in and tied up at the other end of the dock.

"I say there, young fellow, mighty nice salmon you have aboard."

At the sound of the voice with a strong English accent, we looked up to see a naval officer peering down at us from the edge of the wharf.

"Good fishing, eh?" the friendly speaker went on. "I've been trying to catch a bloody salmon for six months."

After a few more comments concerning fishing and noting that we were Americans he surprised us with, "Come over to the base for tea at four o'clock." Without waiting for an answer he left.

"Tea!" Stu exclaimed a bit dubiously.

"Do you think he expects us?" I asked in astonishment.

"We'll be busy." Dismissing the question he proceeded to

cut a fresh bait.

Later that day we moved from the docks and were fishing a half mile offshore. At ten to four a small navy launch sped swiftly across the water toward us, eased alongside and one of the two sailors greeted us briskly.

"The Captain wants you to come for tea."

"Right now?" Stu said.

"Yes sir. We'll take care of your boat," the sailor replied.

"But I can't go like this," I stammered, indicating my rumpled clothes and grubby shoes.

"Why can't you?" Stu interrupted. "Let's go."

"Captain expects you just as you are, Ma'am, come aboard," and the young sailor held out a hand to assist me.

With our skiff in tow and me hanging onto my straw hat the launch picked up speed and soon we were debarking at the navy dock. One of the sailors escorted us to headquarters where we were greeted by the officer who had spoken to us earlier in the day. He was a short, stockily built man with a round ruddy face, dark shaggy eyebrows, and a dignified but pleasant demeanor. He introduced himself as Commander Windeyer and led us to a room where several officers were relaxing over tea.

Hesitating a moment before introducing his fellow officers, he glanced at Stu's army fatigues which bore no insignia. A discerning man, he quickly and diplomatically said, "This is Captain Neely." With a shrug of his shoulders Private Neely yielded to rank and for our remaining three weeks he willingly answered to "Captain Neely."

A witty man, unassuming and friendly in spite of his military background and stern manner, Commander Windeyer commanded this British Naval Operation. He and his next in command, Lieutenant Love, had seen extremely rough action in the Battle of Crete and were now assigned to inactive duty.

"I would very much like to go fishing with you," Commander Windeyer ventured after a congenial half hour. "Would it be a bloody imposition?"

"Not at all," Stu responded, "Be happy to take you out."

At the agreed time the next day we arrived at the navy dock. The Commander chose to fish with Stu in our borrowed skiff, and to make sure he had his guide's undivided attention, Lieutenant Love was delegated to accompany me in another rowboat. A pleasant fellow and good company, he took his assignment cheerfully although he wasn't the least bit interested in fishing.

Commander Windeyer caught two good-sized chinooks

37

(called kings in Alaska). My husband told me later his companion was so delighted he leaned forward several times to pat the plump silvery salmon lying at his feet.

From that day on we were frequent guests of the Royal British Navy. Almost every day the launch would come racing out before lunch, tea or dinner time.

"The Commander sent us for you," was the young sailor's message. We dined at a long table lined with ten or twelve prim officers in navy blue and lots of gold braid, Commander Windeyer at the head of the table, Stu seated at his left and I between two officers on the opposite side. They were most hospitable people, accepting us regardless of rank and our sometimes less than tidy outdoor clothes.

"They're interfering with my fishing," Stu remarked in all good humor one day watching the approaching navy launch churning up the water. "I'd rather fish than have tea."

"Not me," I stated emphatically, "I'm not likely to ever again have tea with so much brass!"

One day when it began to rain lightly, the launch appeared again.

"The Commander said you might need these," and we stood dumbfounded while the sailors handed us sheepskin coats, hip boots and sou'wester hats. Certainly we would have gone to the bottom had we fallen overboard wearing all that paraphernalia, however kind the intention.

One afternoon a few days before the end of our vacation, we were cleaning the day's catch on the beach when I looked up to see the hotel man in the English tweeds coming towards us.

"Look who's coming," I said in a low voice. Stu glanced up briefly and went on gutting salmon. I noticed the gentleman kept one hand in his coat pocket as he approached us.

"Good luck today, eh?" he commented. Stu gave him a short grunt without looking up.

"They tell me you're quite a fisherman," he said, making another uncomfortable attempt at conversation.

When there was still no response, he abruptly pulled his hand out of his pocket holding a slimy herring and with a sheepish look on his face asked, "Would you please show me how to cut bait like you use?"

My fisherman couldn't keep a straight face any longer. With a grin he held out his hand for the herring.

The day before we were to return home, a navy officer drove off with our car and when he brought it back we found the gas tank full, this at a time gas rationing was in effect. There was also a case of ale, choice Canadian cheese and other gifts in the car.

It was with gratitude and satisfaction for a vacation well-spent, we said goodbye to our new-found friends at the navy base, the local people and the couple who had so graciously opened their home to us.

"Well, how about it?" Stu asked as we drove south. "Do you think you'll like fishing in Alaska?"

"Oh yes, I'm sure I will," I answered. Not exactly what I had planned two years earlier but now that didn't seem to matter.

4

Pelican

There was never any question in the mind of either of us as to our future plans — we were both anxious to return to Alaska. And, because Stu wanted to have a try at fishing commercially with sport-fishing gear, an unheard-of achievement, southeast Alaska with its sheltered inland waters was ideal. I was willing and content to go along with his plans, which would be new experience for me.

"Let's hurry to Seattle and book passage on one of the ships," Stu said after his discharge from the service in California in April of 1946. We were amazed to find all passage booked up for weeks ahead except in steerage. There was still a lot of traffic due to military activities, people returning to the territory to live and the greater than usual influx of job seekers.

"How will we get back?" I felt momentarily helpless at the sudden setback in our plans.

"If you don't mind I'll go steerage," Stu said, "and you try to get on a plane. You may have to wait a while."

"Isn't steerage awful?" I asked thinking of tales I had heard in the past.

"Oh no, not at all," he replied, smiling. "You've read too many stories. In steerage meals are served more like boarding house style and I'll sleep deeper down in the ship or near the engines. That's the only difference, besides being less expensive. I can go on other decks just like the other passengers."

"All right then," I said, becoming optimistic, "I'll sit in the Pan American office hoping for a cancellation."

Stu took along some of our personal belongings as baggage but all of our household goods and fishing gear had to be shipped by freighter. I went to a hotel and early the second morning I was on hand when there was a cancellation on a flight to Juneau. It was an eight-hour flight on a two propeller plane. When Stu's ship docked a day later, Fern and I were standing on the dock.

A friend who was a fish buyer in Pelican had offered Stu work for the summer. Since we had no boat of our own yet, he accepted the offer hoping to do some salmon-fishing after working hours. As it happened, our freight did not arrive until the summer was half over, due to some mix-up or delay.

Always ready to make a deal, my husband had bargained for our passage on the mailboat from Juneau to Pelican, a one-day trip. Stu took a turn at the wheel while I cooked two meals aboard for five passengers and the skipper who kept finding excuses to go, he said, to the engine room. Stu wasn't familiar with the route so asked me to take the wheel while he looked for the skipper who had been gone an unusually long time. Stu found him sitting on the john sound asleep.

It was late afternoon when we arrived at the small fishing village. Pelican was west of Juneau on Chichagof Island, built on pilings in the shadow of steep mountains bordering Lisianski Inlet — a narrow but deep channel perhaps twenty-five miles in length. Weather-beaten buildings stood on each side of the wide elevated boardwalk that followed the curve of the beach from one end of town to the other. There were a few cottages, some shacks, cannery cabins, and a bunkhouse, all built on pilings or wooden frames over rocks and an impenetrable growth of brush and evergreens.

The docks, a huge fish house and cold storage, a cannery and a general store formed the business center of Pelican at the north end of the boardwalk. At the other end several acres of tide flats provided the only level ground available. We later discovered this was the baseball field.

"High tide, no baseball," I once heard a Filipino cannery worker mutter as he passed by me.

Pelican had no room for roads, no need of cars, and no telephone poles. However, there was radio communication, a mailboat once a week and small plane service. Freighters brought in supplies and left with tons of canned or frozen fish.

Living quarters were scarce in the summer time; even the shacks were occupied. Frank and Blod Mosier, the fish buyer and his wife, offered to share their two-bedroom rented house with us. The Mosiers were often at their office bargaining for fish until late in the evening so sharing a bathroom, kitchen and dining room presented no problems. There were several buyers, representing big companies in the States, and the business was highly competitive. A buyer usually cinched a deal by passing around drinks to the fisherman and his crew from a bottle kept under the desk for this purpose, and how generously the drinks were dispensed might sometimes be a deciding factor.

"If you want to work part-time, you can help me at the office," Mrs. Mosier suggested. "We'll eat together if it's agreeable with you."

We had a very pleasant relationship with the Mosiers, enjoyed visiting and later when there was more time, we canned salmon together. I prepared most of the simple meals on an oil range which also provided heat for the small roughly-built building furnished with the bare necessities, originally intended only for summer occupancy. The few people who lived permanently in Pelican had comfortable homes, some were company-owned and provided for their employees.

Stu worked in the cold storage plant, much of the time in temperatures from thirty to forty below zero in the glazing section. There frozen salmon and halibut were dipped repeatedly into a large vat of water until coated with a layer of ice, then stacked like cord-wood. The men took turns working in other sections of the cold storage where the temperature was not so cold.

"Did you notice," Stu asked one day, "that I can go three days without shaving since I've been working in cold storage?"

The little village bustled with activity, sometimes most of the short night. Fishing boats docked intermittently, followed by the clang and grinding of machinery unloading tons of salmon and halibut. There was constant bantering and good-natured exchange of fishing talk among the fishermen as they hurried to reload supplies and pick up mail. For those so inclined, there was always the welcome distraction of spending a little time in the saloon before shoving off for another hazardous and exacting ten days on the unpredictable sea.

More and more I felt that I was a part of this north country as I lived and worked on the waterfront, absorbing the various expressions and terms so foreign to me. I walked through the big buildings where men were constantly washing down the heavy plank floors where fish were iced or piled until processed. An odor, not unpleasant, of fish mixed with that of tarred piling permeated the air.

After the seasonal work was over we stayed in Pelican another month and I went deer hunting with Stu. We crossed Lisianski Inlet in a skiff and climbed the steep mountains until we were above timber-line, which is at a much lower elevation than farther south, like in Washington or Oregon.

"It's just a little farther," Stu coaxed when I tired and lagged behind. I had discovered that he took it for granted that I could go anywhere he went. I was pleased with this opinion most of the time, but, when tired and grumpy, I resented putting on a tough front instead of receiving sympathy. But in no way would I admit to any weakness.

Breathless when I reached the top, I gazed for long moments at the great expanse of rugged mountains, the highest peaks topped with a fresh icing of snow. I felt well repaid for the rigorous climb, my jaded spirits and injured pride forgotten.

Going down the steep slope with a deer was easy and after several trips we went back to Juneau with four large fish boxes full of frozen venison. Each piece had been dipped in water until coated with a thick layer of ice to prevent thawing on the long day's journey aboard the mailboat.

"That will get us through the winter in good shape," Stu said, after we had packed the meat into rented lockers at a butcher shop in Juneau.

"Along with our summer's wages," I added.

When George Baroumes, owner of the Imperial Cafe, suggested we winter in his cabin "out the road," we readily accepted.

"I'd like to have someone in it and I'll take you out in my car," he said. "There's good clam digging down on the beach, too," he added. "I'll buy two or three gallons a week for the restaurant if you'll bring them in."

"Good deal, we'll do it," Stu replied.

We wasted no time moving into the small but comfortable log cabin fifteen miles out of town on the capital city's longest stretch of road, twenty-five miles of gravel road. Any place beyond the city limits was referred to as "out the road."

Nestled among large hemlock trees, the sturdy two-room cabin boasted running water piped down from an ample spring on the hillside behind it. A wood stove provided warmth and a Coleman gas lantern and coal oil lamps substituted for electric lights. Cleaning the blackened chimneys brought back memories of the days when as children my sisters and I quarreled over whose turn it was to do the hated chore. Now it seemed a minor nuisance and soon we were comfortably settled in our small but cozy log cabin. I was never happier.

5

Clam Digging

Alaska has some of the highest tides in the world. In the Juneau area the range is from minus four to twenty-one feet high. An extreme tide will range from one to four feet below the zero reading and is known as a minus tide. For nearly a month we were busy getting ready for the winter. Stu cut wood and built a smokehouse to smoke venison ribs and hams from the hind quarters. I baked bread once a week and washed clothes on a washboard. Heavy snows came early but we had already found good clam-digging grounds.

"Let's dig clams for the restaurant tonight," Stu said one evening after supper. "There's a four-foot minus tide."

"But I'm so warm and comfortable in here," I grumbled, "and besides I'm reading a good book."

"It's a quiet night. Will do you good. Come on and dress plenty warm," he advised.

"O.K." I agreed, "guess the book can wait." Even digging clams in the middle of the night sounded like a challenging adventure.

Shortly before midnight we tramped through three feet of snow from our cabin to the beach, some 300 yards away. We slid the skiff across the sand to the water's edge, climbed in and rowed a short distance to a tiny island. The outline of the wooded isle was just a shade darker than the sea surrounding it. Because of the minus tide, the beach was wide and bare, the snow above the high tide line barely discernible.

When the boat scraped on the gravel we clambered out and dragged it a little farther up the beach.

"You hold the lantern and I'll do the digging," Stu directed.

After digging a couple of test holes he found a patch of large white clams, so thick and close together we soon had a gunny sack over half full.

"Just like digging a hill of spuds," he remarked.

"Looks like grocery money to me," I added eagerly.

When two more patches produced a similar amount each, we loaded them in the skiff and Stu rowed back towards our sandy shore. There was not a star in the sky. I felt a hint of fine snow brushing my face, already tingling in the frigid air.

"Hear that?" he paused with the oars above water. Faintly I heard wolves howling far away. Although always entranced when I stood outside in the bitter cold listening to the lonesome cries, they often gave me goose pimples. Shivering, I urged Stu on.

"Let's get home before the wolves get closer."

The rhythmic dip of the oars continued. I held the lantern higher, gazing intently into the dark night, expecting to see the sandy beach at any moment.

Suddenly the skiff scraped on rough gravel, not sand!

"What the hell?" Stu exclaimed. "Where are we?" Then. "Well I'll be darned," he muttered. "We didn't go anywhere. We're right back at our diggings."

"What happened?" I asked in bewilderment.

"I guess we made a complete circle. Never did that before. Beats me." Thoroughly disgusted he shoved the boat back into the water.

"Maybe I can do better without the lantern. Set it on the floor behind one of those sacks," he said.

Uneasily I looked into the dark void beyond the island. What if our circling had taken us out there? Could we have found our way back?

Watching more carefully this time, Stu kept the dim outline of the island directly behind us and soon we were unloading on the sandy beach below the cabin. We pulled the skiff up a safe distance, then I led the way up the narrow path with the lantern, Stu following with a sack of clams. Our legs made long grotesque shadows on the snow.

Minutes later we warmed our hands by a crackling fire. I put on a pot of coffee and fixed us each a hot venison sandwich while Stu packed up the rest of the clams from the boat and dumped them in washtubs. He had first rinsed them off in a bucket outside.

"Now the real work begins," he commented. "Just as well get started." Moving his chair next to a tub of clams, he rolled up

45

his sleeves.

"Should finish shucking these in a couple hours."

"Be with you in a minute," I promised. Earlier in the day I had baked a batch of bread and had kept a portion of the dough for cinnamon rolls.

"These will be ready to bake in an hour, then we can have a hot one with our coffee," I said, spreading sugar, cinnamon and butter over the flattened dough.

"Sounds good, hurry it up," Stu urged, smacking his lips. I put the remainder of the lunch-meat outside in a screened box, nailed high up on the wall out of reach of small varmits.

"We'll need more venison from the locker tomorrow," I reminded Stu. We were near enough now to the city to keep our meat in lockers but later, a hundred miles away, we would miss this luxury.

"I'll set the radio close by," I said, "There's no Northern Lights tonight so we should get good reception from Outside."

I don't pretend to fully understand the phenomena of Aurora Borealis, however, simply put, the Northern Lights are produced when gas particles in the upper atmosphere are struck by solar electrons trapped in the earth's magnetic field. All I'm sure of is when these strange lights are visible, virtually all radio communication and reception is cut off because of the electrical activity. Not often are the conditions just right for a display and certainly not on this, a cloudy night.

I pulled my chair alongside the other tub and we went at it, prying the clam shells open one by one and dropping the meat into gallon jars. So far that winter the minus tides had been at night but I really didn't mind although I complained. I wouldn't have missed those nighttime jaunts for anything. The titilating apprehension aroused by furtive glances into the darkness beyond the glow of the lantern, the mystery of nighttime noises and the exhilaration of wind and snow on my face only deepened my attachment to the life I had chosen in the northland.

Often we listened to our battery-powered radio long after midnight when the reception was at its best and the only time we could get Outside stations. The warmth from the cheerful fire, the low friendly hissing of the gas lantern, a hot cup of coffee and good music made our work less tedious and the hours passed pleasantly.

Before I realized how much time had gone by, Stu yawned and stretched his husky frame. His blue eyes under shaggy brows reflected the lamp light.

"That's the last one," he said. "It's four o'clock. I'll clean up

46

the mess then we'll rest a bit before we start for town."

By five-thirty we were on our way, each carrying a packsack loaded with the jars of clams. It was snowing lightly and was very dark; daylight did not come before nine-thirty or ten in mid-winter. Using a flashlight we followed the path, about 100 yards, to the ploughed-out road. The bank of snow on each side outlined the road so we needed no light. Our rubber shoe-pacs broke the silence with soft crunchy sounds.

After a three-mile hike to the Auke Bay grocery store we boarded the early bus along with more than twenty others who lived out the road and worked in Juneau. About half of the riders were government employees. A few were fishermen going in to tend their boats and gear in the small-boat harbor. Others worked at various stores, offices and services typical of any city. Government employment and fishing were now the main indus-tries in this city of nearly 6000. The A.J. gold mine had shut down in 1944, when it could no longer operate at a profit because of the increasing cost of labor, low grade ore and low prices for gold.

In less than an hour's ride we were in the city. Traffic was beginning to stir on the well-lit street in the center of town, while store keepers swept the freshly fallen snow off the sidewalk. Neon lights blinked on one by one as a few people hurried to work; others headed for their favorite cafe at a more leisurely gait. The prevailing coffee-up habit in Alaska served as a time for social and business mingling, relief from a hang-over, or an excuse for dilly-dallying. People greeted each other by name even from across the narrow street. I liked the small town friendliness.

A taxi pulled up to the curb near us, picked up a native Indian couple waiting there and drove down the street two blocks. We watched it make a U-turn, come back one block and stop. The couple climbed out, paid the driver and went into a small cafe just across the street.

"Must have cashed a government check and still have a few dollars left," Stu said.

"Oh, don't be so cynical," I chided in good humor. "Maybe they had a good fishing season and saved their money."

A large short-haired, stockily-built dog ambled across the street just before we reached Gastineau Avenue, where the cafe was located.

"There goes Patsy Ann," Stu said. "Must be a boat coming in, she's headed for the dock."

Patsy Ann was owned by a private family but was the favorite of all Juneau. Although deaf and unable to bark she somehow knew when a ship was entering the harbor and never

47

failed to meet it at the dock. Her faithful appearance was always rewarded by a handout from the galley.

"How in the world does she know?" It was more of a puzzled statement than a question. "I've heard some say she detects the vibration from the ship's whistle, but she's been seen either on the way or at the wharf even before the whistles blast."

"Beats me," Stu replied, shaking his head.

The well-lit cafe to which we delivered the four gallons of clams was crowded and noisy with a cheerful, friendly atmosphere. A juke box belted out one of the top ten tunes.

"Bring me more when you can," George said as he handed Stu sixteen dollars. "I have three orders for a fried clam breakfast already."

"Let's splurge on a good breakfast," Stu suggested. "I'm hungry."

"So am I," I said, hurrying to a vacant booth. While we ate, the president of the bank where I worked before I married stopped by and had a cup of coffee with us. On his way out he stopped to visit a minute with a couple of dock workers sitting at the counter. Again I was glad to be in Alaska.

We stopped by to see Fern and two-year old Susan a few minutes then visited around town and shopped for groceries to fill our packsacks before returning home late in the afternoon. Shortly after moving into the cabin we had brought in a supply of bulk groceries with the help of an acquaintance who owned a pickup and lived a few miles beyond us. We stored the staples in large empty lard cans that we had bought from the bakery for a few cents each. So unless we wanted to go to the city for social or other reasons, one or two trips a month was enough to obtain extra items needed or to get venison from the locker.

Twilight, only a brief interval between darkness and daylight at this time of year, was closing in on the short day when we trudged up the path to our cabin. More snow had fallen.

"I'll build up the fire then shovel the snow off the roof before dark," Stu said. "Don't know how much more there might be before morning."

I slipped off my boots and flopped into a chair. "I'm tired."

"I'm sure you are," he replied. "No clam digging tonight . . . you can sleep in tomorrow morning."

That was what I was doing, soundly, hours later when I was awakened by a loud "Hit the deck! I'm hungry."

I stirred enough to look out the window near the stove. It was bright daylight, which meant ten o'clock or after, but the window next to the bed was still covered with frosty sculpturing.

"Just a little longer," I mumbled pulling the blanket over my ears.

"I'll give you three minutes or out you go in the snow."

Ignoring the threat, I luxuriated in the combined warmth of the bed and fire and the aroma of fresh coffee.

Exactly three minutes later I was unceremoniously dumped into the pile of freshly shovelled snow, arms and legs pointing heavenward.

"I won't ever dig another clam," I sputtered, floundering in the icy snowbank.

Despite these startling occurrences that I hadn't bargained for, life was good. We had good health, plenty to eat and enough social life to keep from being bored. I felt I had more than my share of happiness.

A few days later we were reading and enjoying a rare evening of good radio reception when I laid my book down muttering in disgust about nature's ill-timed calls to the outhouse. I slipped on a jacket and lined boots and started for the door with a flashlight.

"Here, take the gas lantern," Stu said. "It's warmer. I can sit in the dark awhile."

He was sitting by the stove with his feet on the open oven door whittling on a chunk of jerky with his pocket knife. As I went out the door he turned the battery-powered radio up louder.

The night was pitch black, not a star in sight and the temperature was close to zero. I felt a little warmth from the lantern but did not tarry long. I had just picked up the lantern to hurry back to the house when I heard a shuffling in the snow. Then something bumped against the outhouse, followed by a few grunts, and continued moving slowly and low down around the slight building.

A bear? They're supposed to be asleep, I thought. Then I recalled hearing or reading that bears sometimes make a grunting sound. I drew a shaky breath. If I pounded on the wall or yelled would it make the bear mad, if it was a bear? And would Stu hear me above the radio and with the door shut? I was getting chilled but that wasn't the only reason I was shivering.

The grunting had moved to the back of the privy now and I had just about decided to make a run for it, swinging the lantern around me, when I heard Stu holler.

"You sleeping out there?" The grunting stopped. Opening the door a few inches I yelled. "There's something out here. I think it's a bear."

A minute later Stu came up the path playing the beam from the flashlight on either side of the tiny structure. Then all at once

49

he started laughing.

"Come on out, it's just a porcupine. You're safe."

"It's not funny!" I said indignantly, when I was warming myself by the stove again and heard Stu chuckling.

"Okay." He glanced up at me from his chair, but I could see the laughter still pulling at the corners of his mouth and finally I had to laugh too.

The usual heavy rains held off as winter passed and the snow was slow to leave. On a blustery day in March I was curled up by the fire with a book when Stu came busting into the cabin.

"Your lazy days are over," he announced cheerfully. "We're going to work!"

"What do you mean, we?" I said flippantly. "I wasn't looking for work." I laid my book aside, stood up and stirred the pot of beans that simmered on the back of the stove. I wasn't sure yet if he was serious or just teasing me.

"I saw John Willis at Auke Bay," he said more seriously.

"Who's John Willis?" I interrupted.

"A friend I worked with when I first came to Juneau," Stu answered. "He's going to put in a herring pot out here in the bay right near the beach where we dug for clams."

"The beans are ready and the cornbread is done," I said opening the oven door. "Let's have a bite to eat while you talk me into going to work."

Stu explained that the herring pot would be built alongside John's sixty-foot boat anchored in the bay. When the halibut season opened about the first of May, the halibut fishermen would buy herring from him for bait. There would be a crew of four men, including Stu, and I would cook for them on the boat. Stu and I could sleep at home and the others on the boat.

"Well, what do you think about it?" he asked after we had finished eating and I poured a second cup of coffee. "I haven't given John a definite answer yet."

"I've never cooked on a boat before," I said, "But that shouldn't be a big problem."

"This will only last a couple months," he said. "We'll be through in time to start salmon fishing."

"I'll go along with you," I agreed. "I think it will be an interesting experience." Then I added, thoughtfully. "It seems like winter went awfully fast."

Henry Museth and Charlie Mackey, both experienced boatsmen, made up the remainder of the crew. The men worked for weeks in rain and snow flurries constructing a large circular enclosure of fine-mesh netting, supported by many buoys. I kept hot coffee ready on the oil-burning stove in the boat's galley. Like most fishing or work vessels, a minimum of space is sacrificed for living quarters. A table with a raised edge, especially built for boats, served as a dining table as well as my work counter.

Stu and I usually went home after the evening meal until the construction was completed.

"Now how are you going to get the herring to go in the pond?" I asked him one evening, not wanting to reveal my ignorance in front of the other men.

"During the spawning time in the spring, the herring runs are close to the beach for several weeks," Stu explained. "We'll stretch an arm of the net out and that will turn the herring into the pot and when it's full we'll close the gate."

The opening of the halibut season brought warmer weather, hectic days and irregular hours. Many times there were eight or ten vessels moored side by side against John's boat waiting their turn for herring. Power machinery lowered a braill (net basket) into the pot, lifted out several barrels of herring which were dumped onto the first halibut boat in line. After paying for his bait, the skipper quickly slipped out of the line-up and the next boat moved alongside.

There was the usual good-natured bantering among the fishermen but time meant money now and they all hurried on their way, the crew of each boat starting at once to bait their hooks with the fresh bait.

There were leisure times when there were no customers and the pond didn't need replenishing; short intervals when we could try for one of the big kings that followed the herring into the bay. No one objected to being served many meals of the delicious salmon since our pay was on a percentage basis after groceries.

An occasional session with the fishing pole and the feel of a bucking king at the end of the line had us both wanting to get started fishing steady, not the least attraction of which was the provocative guess at the dollar-value jerking desperately on the thread-like line.

6

Stormbound

We paid the sum of one dollar for our first commercial salmon fishing license. For fifty dollars we bought an old sixteen-foot flat-bottom skiff with a ten-horse motor and with our bamboo poles and a landing net we were in business. We rented moorage for our skiff at Donohue's Float in Tee Harbor, a well-sheltered harbor five or six miles north of our cabin. Early in the spring, while working on the herring pot, we had our 1941 Ford coupe shipped to Juneau by the Alaska Steamship Company. The vehicle provided us with transportation and a means to haul our salmon to Auke Bay or Juneau fish-buyers. We had bought the car while Stu was in the service and had stored it at his brother's place in Auburn, Washington.

A year later we had prospered to the extent that we could replace the plank skiff and old motor with a new 25 horsepower motor and a sixteen-foot V-bottom open boat, a Reinall, which we bought for $300 from the owner of the float, Jack Donohue. I was elated. We were traveling in class now in a beautifully designed vessel that rode the waves like a sea gull. Not yet fully at ease on the water or familiar with the changing moods of the sea, I felt much safer and comfortable, too. The decking over the bow provided a dry place to keep our lunches, extra jackets and other necessities.

The old flat-bottom boat had given us many a rough ride, slapping the water until I thought my teeth would surely jar loose. If the sea was at all choppy we wore slickers to protect us as the heavy craft ploughed into the waves, dousing us with the cold water. I licked at the salt on my lips while bracing my arms against the seat of the old boat. The speedier Reinall enabled us to get to and from our fishing grounds much faster and even to outrun an approaching storm—sometimes.

After considerable prospecting for a promising "hole," we found the area around Aaron Island to be most favorable and productive for us. Only four miles across the channel, due west from Tee Harbor, the tiny heavily-wooded island, ringed by sheer rock cliffs, had a partially sheltered harbor on the north end suitable for small craft only. Wild columbine grew above the small sandy beach where we often ate our lunch and later Stu gutted the salmon there that we caught.

One afternoon at low tide I had walked back to look at the flowers while Stu finished cleaning the salmon. When I turned and started back I saw the boat drifting away from the beach.

"Stu! Look at the boat!" I hollered as I ran toward him. We didn't realize the tide had already changed and the rising water had floated the boat.

Stu took one look, pulled off his rubber boots, heavy shirt and pants, plunged into the icy water and with a few swift strokes swam to the boat.

"I don't understand how that happened so quickly," he said when he was back on shore wringing out his wet clothes and slipping into dry ones. "I just looked at it a minute before."

"Gee, that water must be cold," I sympathized. "What if you had a cramp?"

"I wasn't in long enough to get chilled," he replied. "Besides, what else could I do? We could have been stranded here a couple days and our boat wrecked on the rocks or lost."

"Next time I'll stay with it," I vowed.

As far as we know my husband introduced strip fishing to the Juneau area. His combination of a limber pole, light weight line and freshly cut bait was unbeatable. The scent of fresh blood from the cut herring was a terrific enticement for salmon as well as other fish. By this time, beautiful and durable fiber glass rods had replaced the old bamboo poles.

When we first started fishing at Aaron Island, day after day we were the only fishermen there. On weekends there was a scattering of small open boats, but rarely did we see a cabin boat or even one with a canopy. When we consistently began to unload fifteen to thirty salmon a day at Donohue's float, strip fishing soon became popular. Before long people were not only sport-fishing but earning a few extra dollars on weekends and on the long evenings.

On one of those days when we still had Aaron Island pretty much to ourselves, Stu and I were mooching (drifting or rowing slowly) with our lines trailing from the stern of the boat. Because our motor wasn't running we could hear every word spoken by the four occupants of a motor boat trolling a short distance from us. The voice of the man at the motor came loudly to us above the noise.

"That little woman ain't no bigger than a pint of pee," the voice said, "and that big guy there, that's her husband, and I'll guarantee you'll never catch him on the oars."

Chuckling, we paid no attention to the other fishermen, not wanting to let them know we overheard and spoil our chance for more juicy tidbits. What they didn't know was that I rowed by choice at every opportunity. The exercise kept me warm and it was easy while mooching along slowly. Also I could keep my hands out of the cold water which was part of gutting herring and baiting hooks. I preferred leaving the messy work to Stu.

"Let's make a couple more passes over the hole and call it quits," he suggested a short time later. Since it was late afternoon I readily agreed.

The "hole" was a small area of deeper water where we often hooked a salmon. Just the day before Stu had lost a pole there when a sudden strike tipped it overboard from where he had carelessly laid it across the stern. Most of the time we held our poles, alert to the slightest nibble or tug on the line. But sometimes while cutting bait or relaxing with a cup of coffee, the rods would be propped against the side of the boat with the butt ends on the floorboard and the greater portion inside the boat to keep them from overbalancing. The reel would respond to any pull on the line.

On the next pass Stu reeled one line in and pointing to the other, said, "I'll let this one down to the bottom once more, then reel up and we'll go home." A moment later his rod bent downward and the reel started unwinding steadily instead of in jerks like a salmon usually acts.

"Must be a halibut," he commented, "I was on the bottom." I stopped rowing and we both stood looking down into the water as he reeled in slowly.

"Well, I'll be darned," he burst out in amazement as he pulled up the rod he had lost the day before. His hook had snagged one of the guides.

"I suppose the king didn't stop until he broke the leader yesterday," Stu said. "Maybe I can get some of my line back." Taking the salvaged pole he commenced reeling in. But the line did not reel in freely, it became taut.

"What the heck!" Stu exclaimed. "Maybe the leader didn't

break and the hook is caught on the bottom."

"But it's jerking," I said, getting excited.

"Must have snagged a scrap fish," he said, looking more confused all the time.

Suddenly the reel buzzed and the line moved in a half circle. "That's not a scrap fish," I yelled. "It's too fast!"

"Might be a halibut but it doesn't act like one," Stu spluttered, reeling in frantically as the line suddenly went slack.

"It's coming in," he hollered. Something splashed about ten feet from the boat.

"Get the net!" Stu yelled. "It's a king salmon!" And soon we were staring at the salmon that had pulled the pole overboard.

"That's one for the book!" was his amazed comment.

In the excitement, we hadn't noticed darkening clouds gathering to the southwest. Now a brisk breeze came up and we saw that the other fishermen had already left for Tee Harbor.

"We'd better head for home," I said with alarm, pointing to the south where a dark streak across the water warned of rough water churned up by the approaching storm. Stu took one look and immediately started the motor. We had gone only a short distance when the propeller evidently hit a small submerged piece of driftwood that broke the cotter pin.

"You get on the oars," he directed me, "I have a spare, I'll have it fixed in a minute." But before he could get the tools together and find the extra pin the wind had become so strong and the water so turbulent that it was impossible to install the pin. I was rowing hard but losing ground.

"Let's head for the island!" Stu shouted as he bent over the oars. With both of us pushing and pulling with all our strength we gradually made progress until we managed to pull into the small sheltered nook on the north end of the island.

These sudden squalls were not uncommon in southeastern Alaska, and sometimes calmed down in a couple of hours.

"I'll build a fire on the beach and we'll have a cup of coffee," Stu suggested. "There's lots of time to get home before dark."

But the storm didn't abate. It steadily increased in fury. From emergency supplies in the boat we put a can of coffee to brewing on the fire and ate what was left of our lunch. When it started to get dark we knew we were stranded for the night.

Years before someone had raised foxes on the island. When the price of pelts dropped so low they could no longer make a profit the project was abandoned. A sturdy old house was the only building left.

"Let's take a look at the old house," my husband proposed.

"We'd at least be under a roof."

The doors and windows had long since been taken away and all that remained inside was a large heavy plank table and a grimy, well-worn, old-fashioned couch with a raised headrest. A few foxes had survived and their offspring had returned to the wilderness environment. On past trips to the island we had occasionally caught a glimpse of one before it darted into the brush.

"I'll take the couch," I quickly spoke up. In spite of the lumpy mattress it looked more comfortable than the hard floor.

"All right," Stu agreed. "I think I'll stretch out on the table, it's cleaner than the floor."

We used our hats for pillows and spread our raincoats over us. Lying there I wondered what kind of people had lived here. Was it a man and wife? If so, was she a demanding woman who had insisted on this house built of good store-bought lumber, doors and windows? What an incredible struggle it must have been. Everything, including nails, furniture and stove, would have had to come from Juneau by boat or barge, then transferred to a rowboat or raft and unloaded by hand on a high tide.

Would a man have taken on this terrific task for himself alone? I knew my husband wouldn't have; neither would I have asked for it. Perhaps the man had felt it all worthwhile in return for the companionship of a woman on this isolated bit of rock and timber.

Tired after the long day I soon fell asleep only to be awakened about an hour later by the most awful stench. For a moment I couldn't imagine where it came from—then I realized I was right in the middle of it. As my feet hit the floor a pair of shining eyes in the dark doorway quickly disappeared.

The reason for the terrible smell suddenly dawned on me. The foxes had obviously been using the couch to sleep on and my body heat, along with the raincoat covering me, had stirred up the animal odors accumulated over the years from many foxes. I shuddered.

"Move over," I sputtered, nudging my husband as I crawled up on the table. As I tried to get comfortable I thought of the soft bed at home.

We slept fitfully, and were relieved when at daybreak the sea was smooth. The tangy morning air was doubly refreshing as our little craft skimmed across waters so hostile only a few hours before.

7

A Hunting Trip

"I'll be back for you on Friday," our good friend and neighbor, Ralph Reischal, promised. Then handing me my .32 rifle he paused a moment while looking at it.

"With that pop-gun, lucky for you the grizzlies are holed up for the winter."

"Good luck!" he waved, turned and climbed on board his boat—an army surplus small landing-craft. Backing it out of the mouth of the creek where he had beached it, he headed towards home, fifteen miles across Favorite Channel.

It was Monday of a cold mid-December day in the late forties. Ralph had brought us over to spend a few days deer-hunting at his cabin on the northeast coast of Admiralty Island. He and his wife Treva lived on Fritz Cove Road, twenty miles northwest of Juneau and we rented a small house from them. Their property, located on a sheltered bay dotted with small islands, afforded a safe harbor for their float and boats.

We had moved from the log cabin near Auke Bay because Reishal's float provided a much safer and more convenient moorage for our boat. Also, we had the use of a plot of ground and hoped to raise enough vegetables for our own use. We occasionally indulged in fresh produce on our infrequent trips to the city, but it was all shipped up by boat from outside and was far from fresh by the time it reached the grocery stores.

Standing on the beach we watched a few minutes as the boat spewed out a path of white water behind it. A wisp of smoke escaped the galley stove chimney and hung in the air like a gentle stroke from an artist's brush. The water was unusually calm for wintertime.

"Let's get this stuff up to the cabin and get settled before dark." Stu's urging interrupted a flash of apprehension I was experiencing as I realized we couldn't get off the island even if we wanted to before the agreed-upon day.

"You know, we really are alone," I said, casting a last glance toward the departing vessel before picking up the sleeping bags. "For five days we'll be completely out of touch with the whole world."

"Great!" was his unruffled reply.

Crossing the beach left bare by the high tide, we tramped through twelve or fourteen inches of snow to the rugged little cabin just out of sight under spruce and hemlock trees. Ralph had acquired it from a trapper years earlier to use when hunting. Although weathered gray, the logs were in good condition; bits of the moss caulking had crumbled away but most of it was still intact. A small porch was stacked with dry wood.

Stu pushed hard to open the creaky door stuck tight from the dampness. In the northern wilderness cabin doors are never locked in consideration of a lost or stormbound traveler. The unwritten law requires that the wood used for a fire be replaced if possible.

The scanty furnishings were old but adequate; a variety of utensils hung on the wall behind the small cast iron stove.

"How did they get this heavy stove in here?" I wondered outloud.

"They probably unloaded it from a boat and packed it in by hand, the same way as with everything else," he told me.

Two small bare windows in opposite walls provided light and a view of snow-covered brush and trees, and from one I saw a flash of the shimmering sea between the trees. There was no need of curtains here, nor would they be practical.

"Not even a mouse track in sight," I exclaimed.

"Whoever used it last left it in good shape," Stu observed with relief.

I unpacked the groceries while Stu built a fire in the sturdy stove which immediately started belching smoke into the cabin.

"Forgot to take the cover off the chimney," Stu sheepishly muttered, coughing as he hurried out. He climbed up on the roof and soon the smoke was spiraling up through the tree tops. By the time all the supplies were carried in and other chores completed, the cabin was warm and comfortable. Stu brought a bucket of sparkling clear water from the nearby creek.

"Is the creek frozen over?" I asked.

"Part way," was the answer, "but I didn't have to chop a

hole in the ice and there's still lots of running water."

"One more important chore before dark," I said. "While you pack up more water I'll shovel a path to the outhouse."

"Never mind, I'll tramp a trail out there later," Stu answered.

"I'll do it now," I insisted as I picked up the shovel. "I don't want to be stumbling around in the snow when it's below zero — a clear path for a quick trip is a must."

To my surprise it was dry inside the tiny structure. Remains of a five-year old Sears summer catalog hung from a nail in the wall. I didn't linger long to look at the pictures of swimming suits and summery dresses.

After an early dinner and a walk along the beach darkness closed in on the short winter day. Stu lit the gasoline lantern and hung it on a hook hanging from the ceiling.

Later we talked and read, seated comfortably by the crackling fire, our feet propped up on an apple box close to the stove. At times we shared an interesting article, but mostly we just sat basking in the warmth and coziness. A low steady hiss came from the gas lantern and its glow cast shadows on the walls. My sense of being forlorn and isolated had vanished. Seldom had I experienced such serenity; such a feeling of being where I belonged.

My dreams were becoming reality. Already I knew that life in the north country wasn't all glamorous, nor had I expected it to be so. Even though our income was limited by our small-scale fishing method, I was not concerned; we readily took advantage of the many natural resources around us. My husband just wasn't a nine to five man and although I had supported myself since high school, as well as contributing to a large family, I easily adapted to his mode of life. Many times we had to work hard and put in long hours but the freedom of our chosen way of life was most satisfying. Security could wait.

"Don't move!" Stu's low whisper broke into my reflections and brought my sleepy eyes open.

"The table . . . turn slowly!" I could barely hear him. He was facing the table next to the wall across the room and I had to turn my head to bring it into view. With no idea what to expect, I held my breath while I turned slowly and quietly. Then I saw it! A small snow-white animal with a black-tipped tail was crawling up over the edge of the table. The slight movement I made caused it to scurry out of sight.

"Turn now and get comfortable," Stu whispered, "it'll be back."

"What is it?" I asked, still whispering.

"A weasel," he answered.

I was insisting I had seen weasels but they were brown when he silenced me with a "sh-h." There was a rustle in the corner. A moment later the little mammal appeared on the table again, its beady eyes glittering in the light from the lantern as its glance darted around the room. Furtively it moved about on the table, sniffing at the dishes and groceries; searching for something to its liking — perhaps raw meat. Then stretching to its full length, the long slim prowler placed its front feet on the edge of the full water bucket and proceeded to have a drink. When Stu gave a low whistle our uninvited guest raised its head briskly, glanced about and after another whistle scurried off the table and disappeared. After a moments search, we discovered a small hole in the floor next to the wall.

"A weasel turns white in winter, blending with the snow," Stu explained as we settled down to sleep. "Mother Nature's way of protecting it. When a weasel is white it's called an ermine; the black-tipped tail is the unique feature of the valuable ermine coats."

I had seen many weasels before but never a white one. They are deadly hunters, and we had seen more than one attack an animal many times its size. Fearless, the weasel species belongs to the *Mustalidae* family along with the mink, marten, otter and wolverine, and are considered the most efficient machines of destruction in the mammal world, with a lust to kill even more than they eat. I shuddered. Now I understood why there were no mice in the cabin.

Later that night I was awakened when the unwelcome intruder ran across my sleeping bag.

"Stu!" I yelled, sitting up in alarm. "The weasel is in here! It ran over me!"

"Go to sleep," was his drowsy reply. "It won't hurt you if you don't bother it." Not at all reassured by his lack of concern, I slid deeper into my sleeping bag, pulling it well over my head, afraid to leave even my nose out to tempt the bloodthirsty little beast. Trying to lie motionless, I felt it scurry across my covered head before I finally went to sleep.

Later on, we did enjoy and look forward to the weasel's visit every evening, even luring it with a few scraps, but I insisted on plugging the hole in the floor before going to bed.

On the morning of our third day at the cabin, we awoke to about two inches of newly fallen snow. The tide was low and had not yet washed the beach bare of its white blanket.

"After breakfast let's walk along the beach before the tide comes in," Stu suggested. "If there are any deer moving about we'll see their tracks in the fresh snow."

We had already tried hunting in the brush where the deer might be feeding, and on the muskegs but found it was impossible to wade quietly through deep snow. When we were ready we started out in opposite directions carrying our rifles.

"Stay on the beach and be back at the cabin in an hour," Stu instructed me. "I'll be back too. There's no danger, no wolves on the island and the bear are holed up for the winter." He paused. "But you'd better watch out for the weasels," was his parting quip.

It was a beautiful day. The sky was clearing; the fresh snow covering the trees, rocks and driftwood, glistened and sparkled in the sunlight as if a shower of tiny diamonds had been scattered over everything. I hid behind a log for a few minutes to watch a family of otters playing in the snow, sliding down a snow-covered bank headfirst or rumpfirst, sometimes on their backs, other times on their bellies. They clambered back up to do it over and over again. Occasionally the young ones wrestled or chased each other but they always raced back to the slide.

I went on, then in a little less than half an hour I turned and retraced my steps, allowing myself plenty of time to get back to the cabin at the agreed-on time. Not being intent on watching for deer tracks now, I watched eight or ten seagulls lined up on a drifting log, quietly riding the gentle waves. Others glided and soared until, sighting bits of rubbish or other food at the water's edge, they chased each other towards it and squabbled raucously.

When I was about half the distance back to the cabin I stopped stock-still to stare at a huge track covering my own which was made less than twenty minutes before. Only a bear could make a track like that, heavy and fully a foot long!

"Can't be, they're hibernating," I tried to reason. But it was a bear's! My heart pounded, my hands sweated and my stomach felt like a hard knot as my eyes followed the immense footprints to where they came out of the woods, back-tracked my own a short distance then went back into the woods.

Panic struck me. The next instant I rebuked myself, 'You've got to get a grip on yourself!' I clutched my rifle tight. Noise! That was it, make a lot of noise! We had often beat on cans to scare the bears away when picking huckleberries. So I beat on rocks with a piece of driftwood and yelling my husband's name as loud as I could I walked swiftly towards camp, my voice shrill with fright. I shot my rifle into the air twice, not wanting to use more shells in case I was forced to shoot at the bear, although I knew my little .32 would probably only aggravate it, even if I could stop shaking long enough to take aim. Recalling stories of bears ambushing people, I felt sure the big brownie was watching me from the brush. I had been told that Admiralty Island was the home of an assortment of brown and grizzly bears, the world's largest carnivores. My knees turned rubbery at the thought of being stalked by a half ton of unpredictable fury.

Nearing the cabin I saw Stu hurrying toward me, his .30-06 clasped in both hands. Never was the sight of this big broad-shouldered husband of mine more welcome.

"I saw bear tracks!" I panted when we met.

"I know," he replied brusquely. "Keep moving but don't run. Get into the cabin no matter what happens!"

"Why?" How did he know, I wondered.

"Never mind now," he interrupted. He watched the woods closely as we hurried through the little clearing around the cabin.

"See that?" In shocked dismay he waved an arm. The snow was trampled down all around the cabin by the same big footprints that had followed mine.

Safely inside and trembling, I almost fell into a chair. Stu watched at the window, his big rifle close by. In a few minutes he had unwound enough to tell me what happened when he heard my shots. Thinking I had shot a deer he started back to help me. Nearing the cabin he smelled the unmistakable strong odor of an old bear, not unlike a pigpen, and a moment later he saw the churned up snow and earth left by the rampaging beast — a chilling sight. Horrified, he then thought I must have shot when faced by the angry brownie.

"Why?" I began again.

"Obviously it was mad," he said. "For some reason it hadn't denned up yet. Maybe it was wounded by a hunter or had been some time in the past, and when it got our man scent it went into a rage. Man is their worst and hated enemy."

That night we barricaded the door with the heavy plank table and wash bench. By keeping a fire in the stove and the gas lantern burning all night we hoped that the smell of smoke and the lights would discourage the return of the ill-tempered animal.

"It's likely an old boar came out of his den feeling mighty nasty," Stu remarked. "Sometimes they are just plain mean, especially the old ones, or it might have had a fight with another bear and was already mad when it smelled us."

"Maybe it was sick or had a toothache," I added.

Was it just the night before I had exulted in such peace and quiet?

Old timers told us later that bears do not always hibernate all winter. Some come out occasionally and wander about. Neither of us had seen any sign of deer so we gave up on the hunting and stayed close to camp. Stu chopped wood and beat on a washtub once in a while to discourage our unwelcome visitor.

The weather cleared and turned colder the last night of our stay on the island. I like to think the heavens put on a grand finale for us; a spectacular display of the Northern Lights (Aurora Borealis). Walking to the beach to watch the sky unhindered by the trees, we were fascinated by the twisting, writhing streamers of soft green and white, changing to rosy tinted swirls of light. The streamers undulated into light flame-colored folds that hung from the sky like curtains. At times the ever-changing lights reminded me of the old-fashioned ribbon candy we had at Christmas time.

The beauty of the lights that lit up the sky from horizon to horizon was beyond description. Not until the last streak faded away did we walk back to the cabin hand in hand, strangely silenced by the awesome sight.

Late afternoon of the next day we were waiting with our baggage on the beach when Ralph Reischal arrived. As the boat headed across Favorite Channel we looked forward to getting home but turned for a last lingering look at the little cabin where we spent five unforgettable days. My husband said what we both were thinking. "Wonder if the old sore-head went back to bed?"

8

A Gamble

The winter had passed swiftly and spring was elbowing its way north, swelling the streams with rain and melted snow. It was time to think about plans for the coming months and I still hadn't finished all the reading, visiting and sewing projects I had looked forward to doing.

Then one day, quite unexpectedly, a couple living on Glacier Road offered us an opportunity to operate their farm on a share basis. They had a good market in Juneau for all the vegetables they produced but now wished to retire. We were to provide the labor and could use their equipment. After all operating expenses and supplies were paid for, we would share the profits.

After hours of discussion and figuring, my husband tossed his pencil on the table amid the litter of crumpled sheets of paper and ran his fingers through his dark hair.

"Well, what do you say, shall we gamble on it?"

"We have nothing to lose but work," I replied, "but you know more about gardening than I, so I'll leave it up to you."

"All right! We'll do it! Now let's get some sleep; it's after midnight."

Stu and I were not intimidated by the work that would be involved, both having grown up on farms. However I knew he was somewhat disturbed at the prospect of giving up fishing for the summer. I welcomed the change. It meant I wouldn't need to wear long johns as I had to most of the time in the open boat, and every evening we would be in our comfortable little home overlooking the water. The farm was several miles from where we lived on Fritz Cove Road but was within walking distance of my sister's home so I could see her and Susan often. After fishing, Stu

64

next best enjoyed gardening. The possible financial benefit was an added inducement.

"Anyway," he added cheerfully, "there'll be days we can get away to do a little fishing."

The farm, bordered by brush and small timber, only five miles from the imposing Mendenhall Glacier, had itself been covered by the icy mass at one time. The receding glacier left a sandy loam similar to river bottom earth, ideal for gardening. Much of the terrain in south-eastern Alaska is muskeg, a live mass of mossy-like vegetation mixed with dirt and humus and difficult, if not impossible, to cultivate and build into satisfactory garden soil.

We planted our first onion sets the last week in April and waited impatiently for the unusually wet and cold spring to warm up.

Even then we awoke one morning to see a light snow covering the little green sprouts poking up through the ground. Later we put in more onion sets, but it was the first of June before the radishes, carrots, lettuce and cabbage were planted. As the days lengthened, the increasing hours of daylight seemed to more than make up for the late start, and the vegetables' brisk growth was astounding.

We put in long days cultivating, planting and weeding and were elated over the attractive prospects. We even had time for an occasional day at our favorite fishing grounds. The additional income stretched our dwindling assets, a circumstance that followed a long unproductive winter.

While at work we often heard thunderous roars and looked up to see clouds of swirling snow from avalanches on the mountains adjacent to the glacier. Through glasses we spotted big-horn sheep on the rocky slopes. Once, early in the morning just as we started out to work, we were startled to see a big black bear and her cub in the strawberry patch. They were moving along between two rows, gobbling the berries, green ones and all, from first one side then the other. Not willing to take any chances with a mother bear we quickly moved to the doorway of the barn.

"Get out of there!" Stu yelled after we watched for a few seconds. The surprised creatures looked at us a moment, the berry leaves hanging from their mouths, then bolted for the brush bordering the patch. The old bear nudged the cub from behind so forcefully that it got ahead of its own clumsy feet and made a complete somersault.

By the middle of July Stu was delivering vegetables twice a week to grocery stores in Juneau. The long hours of daylight and

65

abundant moisture meant the produce was large, crisp and mild in flavor. Only potatoes did not do well in this area; they were watery because of the excess moisture. Fortunately we had not planted many.

"Looks like our gamble is paying off," Stu remarked one evening after dinner as we counted the receipts from a lucrative delivery. More and larger orders in the following weeks swelled our egos as well as our assets. We talked about a new car and a trip Outside.

Of special pleasure to me was a patch of sweet peas I insisted on planting. Early in the spring Stu dug several trenches, each about twenty-five feet long.

Our planting was getting underway just at the time large schools of herring were spawning in the little bay near the cabin so I used the eggs for fertilizer. I can still remember the first time I saw this spectacle of nature. The female herring discharges a mass of whitish eggs that resemble tapioca and adhere together with the consistency of thick hardened gelatine. Stu told me that the male herring fertilized the eggs by spreading its sperm over them as the female laid them. The water in the bays, coves or near shore where the spawning took place, would be stirred to a milky color for hours. The eggs would sometimes get to be two to three inches thick on the rocks, seaweed, or anything stationary in the water.

The Indians anchored large branches offshore a short distance and when covered with spawn, loaded their boats. To them it was a much desired food delicacy which they ate raw. I saw children peel off chunks from seaweed on the beach and eat it like candy.

The spawn does not have a strong fish smell and I was told the taste is quite mild, but I never did get up the courage to try it myself. As far as I was concerned, it made much better fertilizer. So, because the words ecology, environment and conservation were then almost unheard of in the north, we gathered tubs full of the herring eggs, peeling it off the beach and rocks in slabs. Scattering the potent fertilizer in the trenches, we covered it with soil and planted my sweet peas. Two months later we had the most profuse and gorgeous blooms I had ever seen. Every second morning I arose an hour earlier to cut the long stemmed beauties, as many as fifty dozen at each cutting. Some stems actually measured up to seventeen inches. Each row of flowers was a different color.

With such an abundance I approached the owner of a florist shop about selling my sweet peas. I noticed the brief look of amazement that flashed across his face as he observed the unusual blooms. He managed to appear nonchalant but agreed to take as many as I wanted to leave on consignment at twenty-five cents a dozen. I learned later that one amorous suitor had a standing order of ten dozen of my fragrant posies every week with which to woo his lady.

But all did not run as smoothly. The last field of lettuce plants we set out seemed to grow exceptionally slowly and developed a jaundiced look. We were puzzled and concerned. The weather was as good or better than for earlier plantings. The seeds were from the same source and the ground had been fertilized with the same barnyard fertilizer as the rest of the fields which produced heads of lettuce so large they looked more like cabbages.

After much scratching of heads, discussion with our land-lord, and investigations, the men went back to the dairyman who had sold them a big pile of manure that had been at the back of his barn. The dairy farm bordered the tide flats and after close scrutiny they discovered that an extremely high tide had flooded the part of the pile farthest from the barn. The last loads had come from that flooded area and had been spread on the field in which the ailing lettuce grew. Without doubt the salt of the sea water was detrimental to garden plants. We lost two-thirds of the nearly 800 heads of lettuce because of it.

But business was brisk and our customers were happy. Most of the tedious work was over by the first of August and we looked forward to at least another month of harvest. Then on the morning of August 12th a heavy white frost covered everything. Dumbfounded, we stood beside the truck loaded for early morning delivery, our gaze moving from one glistening field to another.

"That does it!" Stu exclaimed, kicking at a clod of dirt. "I think I'd rather gamble on fishing."

I was too disappointed to feel angry.

"Looks like the short Alaska season is just too risky for farming," I agreed sadly.

Most of the vegetables were not damaged but the growing season was definitely over. However we had no regrets; it had been a rewarding experience. Financially we estimated our gamble had paid off as well as if we had fished. There was no way to predict what success we might have had fishing, we could only compare it with our previous year's income, which we had topped.

We could head into the winter feeling comfortably secure but the new car would have to wait. I felt a warm glow of satisfaction. Each new experience had proved to be an adventure and my life in Alaska was all I had wanted and more.

9

Census "Out the Road"

Early in the winter of 1949, after we had finished cleaning up our gardening project, we moved again. Moving was not a hectic time of upheaval because we had accumulated very little personal property while renting. We made do with what furniture was provided, sometimes adding a piece or two. Two or three trips with the car to move our belongings sufficed, and all the fishing gear was piled into the boat.

This time we moved to a roomier and more convenient house at Auke Bay, about thirteen miles from Juneau and only a short distance from Hickey's Store and dock where we had access to good moorage for the boat. Our new home was also near Auke Lake where we liked to skate but the unusually heavy snowfall of that winter put an end to the pleasure. Several times we walked the five miles to Duck Creek where Fern, George and five-year-old Susan lived, and with them we enjoyed wandering through nearby areas of semi-swamp land teeming with wild ducks.

It was late March before the long winter gave way to spring. One morning when I stopped in for a cup of coffee with Fern, she asked, "Why don't you apply for the census-taking job?"

"I think that's a good idea," agreed her neighbor, who had just joined us. "You have a car and nothing to keep you home." They both had small children.

"I hadn't even thought of it," I answered. "But it sounds like a good idea. Might be interesting too," I added as an afterthought.

It was too early to start fishing but Stu was painting the boat and otherwise getting the fishing gear in shape. He readily agreed that I should apply for the census work.

69

"We can use the extra cash too," I said, to justify my anticipated project. "With nothing coming in all winter we're getting near the bottom of the barrel."

A car was needed for the out-of-town work, and my having one meant my application was accepted at once. After three days of classes and instruction I was assigned to the area north of Juneau's city limits, extending to Eagle River, which was the end of the main road. Also included were Fritz Cove and Glacier Roads, each several miles long, but only sparsely populated.

"Remember, the initial purpose of the census is to count noses," was our instructor's final advice. It was the first time ever that the questions included information on income and other personal matters, such as the number of bedrooms in a home and whether or not there were inside or outside toilets. He knew we would encounter some opposition and resentment, so was in effect hinting we should use our judgment and some guess work instead of insisting on specific answers to the objectionable questions. I agreed with him and exercised my imagination quite often.

I felt quite officious as I started out with my huge eighteen by twenty-four inch hardback record book. The majority of the families I contacted lived along the highway, or not far from it because of the difficulty of building private roads through the muskeg, the jungle-like undergrowth, or the rugged terrain. Only in a few areas was there rocky ground or good sandy soil.

As day after day passed I found the experience most challenging and interesting. The pay for different jobs was public knowledge. The mine workers' and other laborers' wages started at five dollars a day; the civil service salary ranged between $5,000 and $10,000 per year. A fisherman's income might vary from very little to several thousand, and I learned early not to waste much time inquiring. Most of them were of an independent nature and guarded their privacy well. A few merchants and business men who were on my route had no intention of revealing their income; I didn't blame them, nor did I attempt to make a guess.

"You tell President Truman that's none of his business," one elderly retired couple answered to all questions except their names and their ages which they gave as "legal," which simply meant over twenty-one. I cut that call short.

If someone bristled a bit at the income query, I'd quickly suggest, "Just make a rough estimate—real rough." In a few cases I didn't ask for the controversial information when I detected hostility from the start. But most people were agreeable and cooperative, even seeming to feel a sort of sympathy for the

70

census takers.

One Swedish woman, for instance, knowing I was working their vicinity and having an appointment in town that day, rose early to bake a Swedish coffee cake for my benefit. She filled a thermos with coffee and left instructions with her fisherman husband to be sure to serve the pastry and coffee with sugar lumps.

One day as I approached the fenced-in yard of a nice home on Fritz Cove Road, a large dog came bounding to the gate barking furiously. As I backed off a lady came out smiling, quieted the dog and led me inside. Then she showed me a cartoon she had cut from a magazine of a bare-fanged, snarling dog holding a trembling census lady at bay. She had been watching for me so I wouldn't have to experience the same ordeal. She also put on a pot of tea to serve with delicious home baked pastries. She and her husband had retired from a business in Juneau to this scenic location, overlooking one of the sheltered passages of deep-blue water cradling small islands, heavily forested to the tide line. Anxious that people be in a good mood for the interview, I always looked for something to admire or compliment them on. I had no problem doing so here when I observed the artistic displays of water colors and handicraft in the room.

The day I went up Salmon Creek Trail I stopped by Duck Creek and asked my sister to go along; it was the eleventh anniversary of the day we arrived in Juneau. After arranging to leave her daughter with the neighbor, she accepted my invitation and we drove several miles to where Salmon Creek flowed into the salt water. There we started the four or five-mile hike into the mountains to see the family at the upper end of the trail. The man of the house worked for the power company as caretaker of the dam which held waters from the snow pack and mountain streams. Most of the way we walked a narrow board walk, built by the power company for the benefit of its employees. It was raised several feet above the ground to escape the devils' clubs— wicked thorny plants—the heavy foliage and the rough terrain. We each carried several cans tied together to create noise to avoid taking a bear by surprise.

"Look at those tracks," Fern said uneasily, pointing to wolf and bear tracks in the scattered clumps of snow left along the way.

"I think they're several days old," I said, hoping I was right.

Several times during the two-hour hike we were startled by the sudden flight of a bunch of grouse from within a few feet of our path.

It was a rare sunny day for early April and an enjoyable outing for us, with glimpses of Lemon Creek Glacier and a scenic view across Gastineau Channel to Douglas Island beyond.

We willingly accepted when the wife of the caretaker invited us to have lunch with them and their two pre-school children. Afterwards I wrote the information needed on a sheet of paper (not willing to lug the official book up the mountain) and we stayed to visit a while. Obviously a lonely life for a young woman, she was hungry for company and eager for news of Juneau where they had lived previously and where their children had been born. She expressed a desire to return to the city when it was time for the children to start school, so as to avoid isolation in the winter months. Arriving home in the late afternoon we were tired but satisfied with a day well-spent.

"Here's a cup of coffee for you," my husband offered when I returned home late one afternoon and relaxed in an easy chair.

"Ugh, I can't look another cup of coffee in the face," I replied. "Every place I go they pour coffee. I want to be as congenial as possible to keep everyone in good humor so I drink it all, weak, strong, black, thick and some a bit aged. I even feel dark brown."

The next day after several uneventful stops, I came to the home of Ralph and Treva Reischal at the end of Fritz Cove Road. When we lived in their spare cabin, I had admired the outstanding location, which overlooked a little harbor, with a striking view across the water. Their three children had grown up here.

A good-sized boat and a couple of small skiffs were tied to the dock. Ralph, a big-game hunting guide and all-round outdoor man, had a pet otter that he had caught when it was just a pup. Land otters are easily trained and soon it was following him everywhere, even riding in the pick-up. But it didn't like women and had bitten their daughter several times, though not seriously. Although it had the run of the house, Treva was firm with it and they tolerated each other. I tried to avoid or ignore it while performing my census duties but in an unguarded moment the otter grabbed my arm and punctured the skin in two places. After chasing the animal outside Treva applied an antiseptic and a band-aid and I went on my way.

"One of the hazards of a career woman," Stu sympathized that evening.

Years later while acting as watchman for the Fish and Wildlife Commission to prevent illegal seining near the mouth of the creeks, Ralph disappeared on Admiralty Island. Leaving his wife aboard their anchored boat one day he went for a walk along the beach, carrying his rifle. He was never seen again. After hours of anxious waiting, Treva summoned help by radio and in the days that followed over two thousand people joined the unsuccessful search for the husband and father of an admired and prominent family.

My census taking went on. Strange things kept cropping up here and there among the routine calls. Calling on a lady who had fled Germany during the Nazi regime, I finished recording the necessary information, thanked her and started for the door.

"Aren't you going to ask me about my religion?" she asked in surprise.

"No," I assured her with a smile. "Our government might be asking some nosey questions about other things but it is not concerned with your religion."

Then there was the lady who kept out of sight, not answering my knock on the door. I knew she was inside because I had seen her cross the road ahead of me as I approached in the car. After trying both front and back doors I started back down the path but turned for one more look before reaching the car. Supposing she was well rid of me she moved too soon and I saw her as she passed in front of a window. I immediately returned and, realizing she had been caught, she opened the door and laughingly invited me in.

"Anyone as determined as you are deserves to win," she gracefully yielded.

"I would only have had to come back again," I excused myself.

I had hoped to make this stop and leave before lunchtime but before I could open my big ledger her husband came in and they both insisted I have lunch with them. Detecting strong resentment about the personal nature of some of the questions, such as income and the number of rooms and baths in their home, how could I do much more than count noses in this kindly household?

I was especially saddened by one visit to a family near the beach some twenty miles from Juneau who had no neighbors for several miles in either direction. The middle-aged couple had recently lost their only child, a fifteen-year-old son, as a result of blood-poisoning from the bite of a deer fly. Since we had only a slight acquaintance, I hesitated to intrude on their grief. But I was courteously invited into the well-kept kitchen where the parents and grandmother had obviously been sharing their loneliness over coffee. Quiet and restrained at first, they soon spoke freely

73

of their loss. I felt they hoped the sharing of it would lessen the hurt. I had intended to cut the interview short but as I continued they seemed relieved and eager to talk of things in general, even venturing to look into the future without their boy.

They told of homesteading and building their own home, hauling lumber from town in an old pick-up. Through a partly open door to another room, I glimpsed a braided rag rug on the floor, similar to a small one I had wiped my feet on at the door. I sensed the pride they must have felt in their home and then when they bought their first cow.

There was not a word about long winter evenings spent by the light of coal oil lamps, of Saturday night baths in a galvanized washtub by the open oven door of the kitchen stove, of pumping water by hand on washday, or of thawing the pump with a teakettle of hot water on a cold winter morning. Instead they spoke of watching the deer and otter and of hearing the wolves howl. They told of their garden hacked out of the wilderness, of wild flowers and the first fresh salmon in the spring. Could these people regain the contentment they had found before in their self-sufficient way of life? I hoped so.

More than an hour had passed before I reluctantly bade them goodbye. Driving back to the main road through mud holes and ruts, bordered by forest and dense undergrowth, I thought of how little most of us know of these unknown people living intensely in their isolated but cherished homes.

One rainy day I was working in the suburbs of Juneau. I had finished the interview with a young lady who was sociable and accommodating. As I left she followed me to the door and stood shaking her head.

"That's my mother next door," she said with a worried note in her voice, "and she's apt to throw you out on your ear."

I hesitated then asked, "Is she opposed to the census?"

"She's rabid about it and she won't use very nice language to tell you so," was the answer.

"Guess there has to be a first martyr to every cause, so here goes." My attempt to be humorous didn't boost my self-confidence one bit.

"Good luck!" was the sympathetic response.

Approaching the house next door I saw a large glass-enclosed porch; although the glass was steamed over, I saw many plants inside.

"I hope I know what they are," I muttered.

Then I saw a hefty dark-haired woman watching me from a window. I swallowed hard. Taking a deep breath I rapped on the door of the porch. With relief I recognized the plants the instant the door opened. Before the anticipated outburst had time to materialize, I exclaimed in obvious admiration, "Oh! African Violets! What a perfectly gorgeous display. You must be an expert, I've never seen anything so delightful!"

The determined face softened; I stepped inside and pointed in wonderment to a particularly pretty bloom. Pleased, she said that was her favorite, identified it by name and proceeded to show and tell me about each plant. I didn't know enough about any kind of violets to ask intelligent questions, but I need not have worried. She did all the talking, happy to have a listener— even the census lady.

An hour and two cups of coffee later, I emerged with what census data I considered expedient, as well as being well-informed on the subject of African violets. As I returned past the first house I saw the daughter's astonished face in the window.

On one bright balmy day I drove into a small clearing. A little old man sat in the sun on a stump near a small, sturdily-built cabin with traces of paint long since faded. Courteously raising a thin bony hand to touch his battered old hat, he made a move to rise but I quickly insisted he keep his seat. I tipped a block of wood upright for myself.

Birds were singing lustily; a humming bird hovered in the air a moment then darted away, its wings creating a whirring hum. The bright fluorescent coloring of the neck and breast feathers glittered in the sun. It was the first one of the tiny creatures I had seen this spring, migrated from as far south as the tropics to nest.

Although most of the surrounding trees were evergreens, there were signs of long dormant brush, ferns and grass responding to springtime awakening.

"Nice little place you have here," I commented after stating my business. "Have you been here long?"

"About twenty-five years, I reckon," he replied, stroking his grayish-yellow beard with a slightly trembling hand.

"Before that lived in Skagway after I come back from the Klondike."

"Did you find gold?" I asked, eager to hear more from this shrunken little fellow of ninety-one years, who I suspected possessed a wealth of memories.

"Enough," he answered briefly, "but it was too rough at the diggings. Come back after a year, winter too damn cold.

His gaze and interest seemed to wander. I felt he was reluctant to talk more or else he was tiring.

"Now what is it you want to know?" he asked lighting up an

75

old corn-cob pipe while looking toward the ledger I held still unopened.

After recording the information I felt was relevant, I couldn't refrain from asking one more question before leaving.

"You live here alone?"

"My grandson and family lives over there," he replied pointing to a small painted cottage on the other side of the clearing.

"Don't worry your pretty head none, they 'hep' me."

I closed my book, thanked him and turned to leave. The old gentleman arose slowly and tipped his worn hat gallantly.

"I won't be here for another census," he said simply.

At last I came to the end of the road at Eagle River where two elderly men lived. They were probably the last of the old hand-trollers. They fished while rowing with heavy hand lines trailing from the stern of their boat.

I parked the car in a wide spot and shouldered the packsack which held my official ledger and a package of homemade cookies and doughnuts. Rather than carry a heavy gun, I preferred my string of noisy cans to prevent an encounter with a bear. Given warning, it will almost invariably leave the vicinity of the noise. There was no possibility of getting lost because I never diverted from a trail or road. Everyone had some manner of access to their homes and we were acquainted with most of the locations. At times Stu would go with me when I was uncertain about a particular road or place.

The sun was shining but there was still white frost in the shade as I followed the winding path for nearly a mile, first through meadow land and then through alder and hemlock trees, some 200-feet above sea level and over-looking Lynn Canal. Stu had sent word by a fisherman friend to the two bachelors that I would be along within a few days, so I did not take them by surprise when I walked into their camp on the beach of a pretty little cove. Each had a tent, only twenty-five or thirty feet apart; their skiffs were pulled up above the high tide line. Fishing gear hung from the branches of nearby trees or lay in orderly fashion and a clothes line strung between trees held several articles of clothing.

"Come on in. It's not much but it's warm inside," one of the men invited in a Scandinavian accent. I was offered the only chair in the tent while one fellow sat on an apple box and the other on his bed. Both men were neat and clean as were the meager but practical furnishings. Both puffed on pipes. I detected the unmistakable odor of fish. A closed kettle on the cast-iron stove

76

caused me to suspect the odor to be a fish stew Scandinavians are very fond of and I had found to be quite tasty.

The inevitable gray enameled coffee pot was on the stove, its aroma competing with that of the fish stew. When one of the men poured three mugs of delicious steaming coffee, I opened the sack of doughnuts. Never had refreshments tasted so good, even in the swanky Baranof Hotel in Juneau, and the earthy friendly atmosphere made them even more enjoyable.

The two old hand-trollers, their hair gray and shoulders stooped from years of rowing, caught and sold enough salmon to live comfortably, each in his own small apartment in Juneau during the winter months. They did not object to the census report even though some of their answers were vague. I saw no reason to mention the queries concerning housing and plumbing.

"You don't need to fear for bears," they assured me as I left, their ruddy weather-beaten faces etched with crinkly smiles. "We heard you coming afar off."

10

The Boondocks

"Time to get back to the boondocks," my husband announced, slipping on his gray 'halibut shirt', a heavy wool combination jacket-shirt popular with halibut fishermen. Picking up a box of groceries and his rifle he went out the door on a cloudy day in late July.

Stuffing the pockets of my coat with apples and candy bars I followed. Experiencing a fleeting twinge of reluctance to leave the comfort and security of our small home—electricity, easy chairs, ruffled curtains—I took a lingering glance inside before closing the door.

I enjoyed our little home set back among the trees, out of sight of the road and yet a short distance from Hickey's country store and the float where we kept our boat. The village consisted of two general stores, a post office, church, a small hardware store and a scattering of homes. Some were fine modern homes on the waterfront overlooking beautiful Auke Bay or nearby Auke Lake. Only five miles inland, Mendenhall Glacier, curving back into the mountains like a frozen river, had provided ice for the ice boxes of Juneau until electric refrigerators put the ice-man out of business.

A humming bird buzzed by me repeatedly.

"Must have a nest nearby," I speculated, knowing that the tiny creatures will on occasion attack much larger birds, even causing hawks to retreat in haste. I held one in my hand one day after it had come in through an open window and I caught it while it fluttered against a window pane. Its soft fluffy body vibrated like a racing miniature motor. I was amazed to find that the long menacing bill was not rigid, as I had supposed, but quite pliable.

A bluejay scolded from a tree as I followed Stu down the brush-bordered path and across the road to the boat landing. Soon we were skimming over the waters of Lynn Canal. The sun broke through the clouds just long enough to reflect on the glistening blue of Lemon Creek Glacier tucked in a mountain canyon a short distance inland. I breathed deeply the incomparable freshness of early morning. The suggestion of discontent I had silently indulged in a few minutes earlier, dissipated like wisps of fog before a quickening breeze.

While fishing in the vicinity of North Island, about twenty miles north of Auke Bay, we stayed in a friend's camp which consisted of a rough but roomy cabin built on a large scow. Now fastened with cables above the shoreline on the mainland, the scow could be floated and moved to other locations as needed. Every third day we would make the run back to the store and docks. I welcomed a night at home.

"All ashore," Stu called out, easing the boat to a stop on the sandy beach in front of our camp. He secured it with an anchor line and took the lead with the rifle as we carried our supplies to the scow, several hundred yards up the sloping beach. Snuggled in the edge of dense woods and straddling a small creek, it rested on pilings, five or six feet high, with steps going up to the door near the back end.

"Let's have coffee and a bite to eat, then go try the fishing," Stu suggested. I liked his idea and soon we set out in the boat again, but we didn't have long to try. Shortly after we started fishing the sky took on an ominous look and a stiff breeze from the southwest rumpled the water.

"Looks like a big blow coming," he observed looking at the gathering clouds. "Reel 'em up, let's get ashore."

By the time we beached the boat, attached an extra line and went back to the camp, the stiff breeze had turned to a howling gale and the restless sea slapped the beach angrily.

"If you hadn't showed so many people how to strip fish maybe we could still be fishing nearer home instead of out here in the boondocks," I complained later, watching the storm from the window.

"It was inevitable," Stu replied reasonably, running his fingers through his dark hair. "Since the war there's been much publicity and better transportation to Alaska, so more people come up. It's only logical that sportfishing would become increasingly popular every year." When we found we could not make fishing pay commercially any longer at Aaron Island where we first started, it became necessary to look for new fishing grounds more distant. North Island was too far for those fishermen from Juneau who had only a few hours or a day at a time to fish.

"At least we're not crowded here," I admitted grudgingly.

Glancing sideways at Stu, I decided to add more cheerfully, "Oh well, we're comfortable. Now how about a cup of coffee?"

While waiting for the coffee to perk I again wandered to a window, this one facing the woods. Startled to see a large dark form moving in the deep shadows along the creek, I beckoned to Stu.

"Come quick and look! I see something moving up the creek!"

"A bear looking for spawners," he said, after a moment. "Let's watch, there may be more nearby."

Soon another brownie forced its great hulk through the thick underbrush, then both shuffled along the creek, moving out of the shadows and closer to the scow. Fascinated, we watched as the largest one lunged into the creek with incredible speed, its front paws extended, but it backed off without a salmon. Both bears watched the water quietly a few moments, then the other bear pounced into the creek, raised its big head, and with a flopping discolored salmon between its jaws, clambered up on the bank. While this bear bit and tore its tasty morsel, the first brownie shuffled into the middle of the creek, stood with its shaggy head lowered and moments later scooped his own fish out of the water with a big paw and set it flopping on the bank. Almost before it landed the huge animal had bounded out of the water and clamped its jaws around it.

The salmon going up this creek to their spawning grounds were pinks or humpies (so called because of their rounded back). Weighing on an average from three to five pounds, they were caught in nets by seine fishermen before entering the streams. Salmon will not usually take a bait when ready to spawn. We were fishing for the larger and more valuable king salmon, referred to as feeders before their spawning time.

"That's all they get," Stu said when the brownies started back into the creek for another helping. "Need to save some for seed," and he opened the window.

"Get the hell out of here!" he yelled.

I saw the humped shoulders, small ears and wide faces as both animals turned their huge heads to see where the sound had come from. Bears have poor eyesight compensated for by keen ears and sensitive noses. The next instant the darker one wheeled and crashed into the brush. The other, with shiny bronze fur, reared its massive bulk up on its hind legs for just a moment, the salmon still dangling from its jaws, then dropped to all fours and swiftly disappeared.

"Aren't they great?" I exclaimed.

"But dangerous," Stu added. I shuddered, I well remembered what Stu had told me soon after we had seen the bear tracks on our hunting trip.

"Was that a black and a brown bear?" I asked.

"No, they were both brown bears. We call them Brownies in Alaska," he replied. "Both brown and black bear roam the forests of southeastern Alaska but they won't live together in the same area. The larger and more vicious brownies chase the blacks away."

"How much do you think they weigh, anyway?" I questioned, intrigued by the huge animals.

"The brownies are the world's largest carnivores and will weigh from 600 to 1500 pounds and measure three to four feet high at the shoulder," he told me.

"But one of those bears was more black than brown," I insisted.

"Their coloring varies. It may range from a dull yellow to dusky brown and even to near black," he explained. "Grizzlies are smaller, from about 400 to 1000 pounds, and usually of a brownish color but may be black or grey. Their fur is really attractive, the light-tipped hairs give it a frosty sheen."

I learned that Admiralty Island, west of Juneau and a hundred miles in length, is considered to have the greatest population of brownies and grizzlies, and a mixture thereof, in the world. Although they all eat meat, including fish, ants, mice, small animals or the carcass of dead creatures, bears are largely vegetarian, feeding on grass, roots, bark and berries.

The magnificent brownies fear no other living thing but man. They supposedly won't attack a man unless wounded or startled, but I do know of several cases involving a brownie, where the only provocation seemingly was just being in their territory. Stu and I have a healthy respect for these great animals, still of sufficient numbers to be a hazard almost anywhere in the woods or brush. We never ventured far from our dwelling without Stu's big rifle, not even for a walk along the beach.

The storm raged all afternoon and all night. Stu checked the boat every hour or two. After dark I went along to hold the lantern for him. The long sloping beach was fairly well sheltered from rough water but because of the tides it was necessary to keep adjusting the lines to prevent the boat from going high and dry or being pounded on the beach.

"There's a Coast Guard boat out there," Stu said in surprise the next morning looking out the window. The storm had slackened and the vessel lay off shore a safe distance. We saw men on deck looking our way with binoculars.

"I bet they're looking to see if we're in trouble," Stu said going out the door. Evidently in passing they had seen our lantern light on the beach in the night and thought someone might need help. Stu quickly signalled that all was well and with a wave they moved on.

Several days later coming in tired and hungry from a successful day of fishing, I picked up the empty thermos and slickers and headed for the house, not realizing Stu was delayed at the boat. Coming to the top of the rise only a couple hundred feet from our camp I stopped short. Between the pilings under the scow I saw furry legs moving around near the steps that led into the house on the far side.

"Look there!" I blurted, thinking Stu was right behind me with his ever-present rifle. No answer. Quickly I looked around. No Stu! I gasped when I saw him still at the boat. Dropping my armload I ran down the beach yelling wildly, "Bear! Bear! Bear!"

Stu grabbed his rifle and raised it to his shoulder ready to shoot, sure there was one right at my heels.

"Where?" he asked. Shaking and panting I could only point to the scow.

"You've made enough noise to scare anything away, but let's go see," he said a bit skeptically but holding his gun in readiness. I followed slowly, a discreet distance to the rear. About halfway to our camp he stopped, raised the rifle and shot into the air twice. I reached his side in time to see four furry rumps disappear into the woods.

"It's getting crowded in the boondocks," my husband commented dryly with a solicitous hand on my shoulder and a mischievous glint in his eye.

After finishing supper that evening I pushed my chair back abruptly.

"Fine Alaskan I am," I bemoaned, "I run at the sight of a bear."

"That's the smartest thing to do if you have time to run," Stu assured me. "You didn't have a gun."

"I like to see them at a safe distance but I know I'll always be afraid of the monsters," I admitted. "Maybe I don't belong up here."

"You'll do," was his typically brief compliment, so sparingly doled out and so eagerly lapped up. Nevertheless, it made me feel better.

In August there were lots of herring for feed and a big run of silvers, a red-meated salmon that averaged possibly twelve to fourteen pounds. We caught twenty to forty-five a day, which kept us jumping during the time of the tide when fishing was good. When the biting slacked off we had time to eat, clean the salmon and rest for a couple of hours.

Stu had made arrangements with a troller who was fishing in the same area to ice and haul our salmon for three cents a pound. We could no longer bring out enough ice or haul that many salmon in our small boat. I believe, at that time, we were paid from sixteen cents a pound for silvers to as much as forty cents for kings, varying according to size and quality.

"Let's roll up the sleeping bags and break camp," Stu said on a day that we were sitting out a blow. "It's the first of September and there'll be more stormy days from here on."

"Good! I've had enough boat rides and fishing for a while," I answered. "It will be nice just to stay home. I'm tired."

I lost no time getting our belongings packed and leaving the cabin ship-shape while Stu loaded the boat. The wind was slacking but he decided we should wait a little longer.

"Just enough coffee left for another cup each," I said, fidgeting around the stove.

"I don't think we'll come back here," Stu remarked as he whittled on a bit of wood. "We've had a good season, more than we would have made with both of us working."

'Doesn't he call this work?' I thought to myself.

"But," he continued, "this is too inconvenient; the long trips, having to carry ice and a chance of losing our salmon if the ice gives out during a storm."

"Not to mention getting clobbered by a brownie," I added. "But where will we fish next summer?"

Stu stretched his arms and yawned.

"We'll think of that next spring," he replied.

11

Angoon

"We're going to Angoon!" Stu announced enthusiastically one balmy spring morning after a mild winter. He slammed the door shut behind him and threw his hat in the corner.

"How soon can you be ready?"

I almost dropped the pan of cookies I was just taking out of the oven.

"Angoon? Where's Angoon? And why and when?" I stammered.

"Relax, you don't have to pack today," he laughed, patting my shoulder with one hand while helping himself to a cookie with the other.

"You know," he continued, "the fishing within reach of home is too crowded now. We're going to have to go farther from the city to make a living."

"But how do you know Angoon is any better?" I asked.

"Jack Manery has fished in the area," Stu answered between bites. "He says there's a place where the hand-trollers can fish close to the rocks and kelp and catch big salmon."

I hesitated. We would have to give up this house, leave our friends and Fern's family. Where would we live? How would we go? How far was it?

"Jack is going trolling over that way in a few days and he invited us to go along on the Hobo. He'll take all our gear and tow our boat. I told him we would go; I hope it's all right with you."

The silence stretched out while his blue eyes studied my face, almost apprehensively. I wondered if he was having second thoughts about committing himself so quickly. I was thinking that he deserved to worry just a little bit for not having discussed it with me first, but when I turned to look at his eager face I knew that I would go! I'd see new country, more of Alaska! Wasn't that why I came north? The uncertainty involved wasn't important anymore; I had experienced that before. Now I had someone to share it with me. My pulse quickened at the challenge of a new adventure!

"Sure, I'll go!" I responded with growing anticipation. "Now where the heck is Angoon?"

The anxious look faded from his face. "I knew you would," he said, almost smugly, giving me a hug and reaching for another cookie.

Fishermen lead a more or less nomadic life, at least during part of the year. The majority have boats with living quarters, a galley and oil stove; they take their homes wherever they go. Some wives go along and help make life aboard more comfortable; some don't like the life afloat, and others work or have responsibilities at home. We were often urged by friends to buy a commercial boat and enjoy the advantage of fishing in safer and warmer conditions. But I realized I was not that much of a sailor; I wanted my feet on solid ground at night and I was relieved when I learned that Stu preferred living ashore too. He would much rather get his fingers in the soil once in a while instead of in the grease of a boat engine. True, we could not equal the income of the larger boats but neither did we have a big investment and, most important, we never lost the fun and thrill of feeling a big salmon jerking on the end of a limber pole.

Three days after the disruption of my placid routine, I had packed large boxes of groceries and the bare necessities for housekeeping while Stu readied the fishing gear and our sixteen-foot boat. We stored the rest of our belongings and our car at Fern's and bid the family goodbye.

"I don't want you to go away," little Susan said hugging me tightly. It was a few seconds before I could answer. We had become quite attached to each other, as she had been born in Alaska and did not know any other relatives.

The Hobo glided out of Auke Bay on a beautiful sunny day, always an added bonus in southeastern Alaska where the rainy days outnumber the clear ones. The homes along the shore, smoke from their chimneys drifting lazily upward, were soon left behind as we crossed the channel and approached Point Retreat at the north end of Admiralty Island.

Chatham Straits was calm as we rounded the point and traveled south some sixty or seventy miles along the west coast of the island. The shoreline was heavily wooded wilderness until we entered the channel leading to Angoon, an Indian village of about five hundred people, the only community on the 100 mile long island.

The rocky shore on each side was lined with dark patches of kelp out of reach of the swift current that flowed in the middle of the channel. On one side perpendicular rock cliffs formed a bulwark for the village sprawling across the high peninsula, and commanded a view of the sea in both directions. Without a safe harbor, boats were forced to anchor farther up the channel where it widened into a sheltered bay. The site of the village was no doubt chosen by the early Indians because of its inaccessibility by sea, which gave it some protection from enemy tribes.

As we cruised up Kootznahoo Inlet, ("Fortress of Bears" in Indian), I wasn't so sure I wanted to be in a small boat in that churning water. The incoming tides flowed up the long narrow inlet to a wide bay covering several square miles. When the tide reversed and the water rushed back out through the narrow opening, it created swift and dangerous currents and huge whirlpools that looked frightening to me. Later we were to see the native children in row boats of questionable sea-worthiness row out from shore to the middle of the channel, then put the oars inside the boat and let the current carry them downstream, spinning them around and around in the whirlpools. Raised on the waterfront they had no fear, even though very few Alaskan children could swim, nor would it have done any good to know how in the icy waters.

After spending a day or two aboard our friend's troller while he visited old friends and Stu sized up the fishing prospects, we decided to look for a place to live. Before Jack moved on to look for favorable troll-fishing grounds, he introduced us to the chief of the Tlingit tribe in Angoon, who welcomed us to the community and agreed to rent us a cabin that he owned but used only occasionally. Since it was across the channel from the village I guessed that it was used when someone went berry-picking or hunting. We found it was not a handy place, but didn't have much choice and we wanted to stay. Stu carefully eased our boat onto the rocky beach and we packed our things over slippery kelp and seaweed. Later he used rocks to form a small reservoir of sorts in the stream nearby, so we could more easily dip out water with a bucket.

The old cabin, which was ten by fourteen feet and made of rough boards, had nothing in it but an old bed with a metal frame, a small table and two old chairs and, to my relief, a good wood stove. The chief and his wife had piled and covered their few belongings in a corner, leaving the cabin neat and clean. However, I felt more like setting up housekeeping after I had tossed a couple of buckets of soapy water over the bare floor and swept it out the open door with my indispensable broom. A crackling wood fire soon dried the floor and warmed my jaded spirits.

"Think we can get along here a while?" Stu asked hopefully while watching me heat up a can of venison.

"Sure, everything will look better after a good night's sleep," I replied, trying to sound more cheerful than I felt. "Anyway," I continued, "housekeeping is going to be simple, just sweep everything out the door."

"Not much of an outhouse out there," Stu said evasively later on in the evening. I paid little attention to his remark, not expecting anything more than an old dilapidated building of some sort. But I stopped short when I followed a faint path back of the cabin, and in the rain, to where a pole was stretched between two trees over a hole in the ground. I turned back to the cabin, flung the door open and stomped inside. I saw Stu glance furtively at me above the magazine he pretended to read.

"I don't mind roughing it," I ranted, "but I'll be darned if I'm going to have the rain running down my back."

"Take it easy, I'll fix something," he said quickly.

"When?" I demanded.

"Right now," he answered, laying the magazine aside. "There's some old boards and a piece of canvas under the porch."

"O.K." I said in my normal tone of voice again. "I'll get the hammer and some nails from our tool box."

Early the next morning we were awakened by the loud rasping of several ravens squabbling over some tempting morsel on the beach. I opened the door just in time to see a mink scurrying from a fruitless search of the boat. The magic restorative qualities of sound sleep and the stimulating freshness of a new day, dispelled all doubts and gloom. I faced the day eagerly.

After a breakfast of coffee and cooked cereal with raisins and canned milk, Stu gathered up the fishing rods.

"Let's go over and get acquainted with the fishbuyer first," he said, "then we'll go see if there are any of those big salmon here that Jack told us about."

"Be ready in a minute," I replied, "shall I make a sandwich?"

"I don't think we'll stay out long today," was his answer, "we'll just sound it out today."

"I've heard that before," I retorted, "I'll make a sandwich."

We found the buyer's sixty-foot boat anchored in the bay at the upper end of the inlet. Jim and Mary, the pleasant, friendly couple who owned and lived on the boat, invited us aboard for coffee. Both were part native and had relatives in the community. Mary had taught school here for several years, but they now owned a home in Juneau. We liked them immediately and were pleased with the helpful bits of information they so willingly gave us. The only other white people in the village were the postmaster and his wife, a young minister, and the older couple Jack had visited. They lived near the airplane float and the man carried the mail the half mile from the float to the village post office.

Fish buyers carry sufficient ice with them to freeze several thousand pounds of fish. Every day the local fishermen sell their catch to the buyer, who will weigh the fish and pay cash on the spot. He ices the salmon in the hold of the vessel for a week or ten days then goes to the city, in this case Juneau, to sell it to fish companies at the cold storage plant. He was paid several cents a pound more than he payed the fishermen on the fishing grounds. At that time we were paid approximately thirty cents for white kings and thirty-eight or forty for reds. White kings are just as good for eating as the red, in fact they are richer in fat, but do not have the market appeal that the red salmon has. Thus the whites are eight to ten cents a pound less, which can make a considerable difference to a fisherman. The percentage of whites to reds vary in different areas for some unknown reason. Near the mainland where we had fished, it was often disappointing to find seventy-five percent of a catch were white. We had heard and hoped that the largest percentage in Chatham Straits were the more profitable reds.

Stopping to jig for a few herring along the kelp bed, we motored down the inlet, avoiding the fearful looking whirlpools by staying in the back eddies near the shore. When we neared Danger Point, a rocky reef that marked the entrance to Angoon, we saw a native hand-troller pulling in a large salmon.

"Jeepers! They are big!" Stu exclaimed. "Let's get at it."

There were ten to twelve hand-trollers, all natives, in double-ended round bottom boats rowing near the kelp and reef to keep away from the swift current. While Stu cut a bait I looked up at a layer of clouds that blanketed the top of the snow-covered mountains on Baranof Island across Chatham Straits. A gentle breeze was coming from the south. I wondered if it would bring more rain with it.

Several hours later we again pulled alongside the buyer's boat, happy and hungry — although the sandwich had helped —with five salmon weighting from twenty-five to forty-five pounds each, and all were reds. From the surprised and pleased look on Jim's face I gathered that this was not an average catch by the skiff fishermen. Smiling to myself, I remembered how he had looked dubiously at our rods earlier but had made no comment.

Day by day, as we learned more about the time of the tides and where to fish, we came in with an increasing number of big salmon, ninety-percent red. Soon we were out-fishing the natives, bringing in more salmon weighing fifty pounds or better than Jim had ever seen caught in this area. Although the chief from whom we had rented the cabin had not lacked in friendliness, we felt a certain hostility from the fishermen. We didn't feel welcome but couldn't blame them, realizing we were outsiders, and most likely considered intruders on their fishing grounds.

"We can bring you groceries from Juneau, or you can buy from the store in the village," Mary offered one day when we came in early because of rough water. "I'm going to the post office now, would you like to come along?"

I hadn't had a chance to talk with any other women since we moved here so I welcomed the opportunity to visit with her.

Stu stayed to talk fishing with Jim while Mary and I went ashore at the plane float, then walked a half mile or so on a trail bordered with salmonberry brush. Children and dogs played in the yards and on the dirt streets lined with mostly unpainted houses. Some were just shacks but others were large and substantially built buildings, looking many years old. Scattered everywhere were childrens' playthings, broken and otherwise, empty cans and bottles. Here and there a few colorful flowers had survived the antics of dogs and kids. Both drab and brightly patterned blankets hung over clothes lines, as well as heavy wool garments, long underwear and gaily printed dresses that re-minded me of pictures from a Sears Roebuck catalog.

Mary introduced me to people we met along the way and to the congenial owner of the store, which was well-stocked with staples, clothes, hardware and rubber boots. He also owned a good-sized seine boat with which he hauled his supplies from Juneau. I knew that regular monthly government checks sup-plemented the inconsistent income of the Indians, whose sole occupation was fishing in one manner or another. Besides the hand-trollers, several of the natives owned expensive seine boats subsidized by the government and a few of the natives prospered. Many of the young fellows worked as crewmen on the local seiners as well as on boats from other communities.

At this time Angoon (meaning "Village at the End of the Trail"), was perhaps the most primitive native Indian village in southeastern Alaska, slow to give up old customs and practices. Not too many generations previously, their aged and infirm were taken out to a rocky reef at low tide and left to die as the incoming tide covered the reef. Superstition played a large role in their daily lives. They would not kill a raven or a bear because they believed their dead relatives returned in these guises. When a big brownie moved into the local graveyard, playing havoc with plots, digging up plants, and eating the wild berries which the natives gathered for food, it was dangerous for everyone in the vicinity. Nevertheless not even the toughest hunter among them would shoot the offending bear. However, they had no objections to calling a U.S. marshal from Juneau to come over and kill the intruder.

We became puzzled and a bit uneasy when we realized that time after time, shortly after we started fishing, the native skiffs circled us then moved up the inlet towards the village.

"Why do they go in every time we start fishing?" I asked Stu.

"I don't know," he replied. "Maybe it just happens that way. They may be fishing a certain time of the tide."

"Looks weird to me," I said, unconvinced. "I'm going to ask the fish buyer when we go in."

When the tide changed the salmon quit biting and we went up the inlet to sell our catch.

"Does it just happen or do the other hand-trollers come in for some reason when we go out?" I asked after our salmon were weighed in and we sat talking.

"We wondered if you had noticed," Jim answered with a smile.

"They believe that little thread you fish with spooks the salmon," he explained, referring to our light weight lines.

Few of the hand-trollers used motors. They fished by rowing their skiffs and dragging a heavy hand line. What we didn't realize was that they had never seen anyone use limber poles and light nylon lines before. However they would in no way indicate that they noticed or were even interested.

"What should we do?" Stu asked seriously. We had no intention of disturbing the community and their fishing procedures.

"Just go ahead and fish," Jim answered. "We're telling them you're fishermen like the rest of us, out to make grocery money."

"Don't worry, they're good people," Mary added. "When they understand they'll accept you."

An opportunity came the next day. Stu was jigging herring for bait with his rod and a line that had several small hooks tied to it about six inches apart. Reeling in while making short jerks with the pole, he pulled in six or eight flopping herring at a time. The shiny hooks resembled shrimp spawn and other minute forms of sea life.

Near us and close to shore a native woman, alone in a skiff, was trying to snag herring by the method used for many generations. A long narrow board with nails imbedded along the edge was quickly dipped into the water, then with an upward sweep and luck a few herring might be impaled. Only when the small fish were quite numerous and near the surface was this crude method successful, whereas Stu's jigging procedure produced results even when the herring were deeper and not visible. The time the hand-trollers spent in the attempt to snag bait meant time lost fishing for the lucrative salmon.

"Let's offer her some herring," Stu said, holding out a gallon can of still-wriggling herring.

"Can you use these?" he called out. Taken by surprise at the generous offer — not often did anyone share the hard-to-come-by herring — she stared at us a moment, then her eyes sparkled and her dark features broke into a big grin.

"I thank you, I thank you," she repeated over and over in a guttural voice reaching eagerly for the can. After that we shared herring at every opportunity.

It wasn't long before the younger Indians became curious when we came in day after day with a good catch of large kings. The natives called them "big slugs." The older natives remained unreachable longer, at least in our presence, but the young fellows looked closely at our gear while we sold our salmon and visited with Jim and Mary.

Our fragile looking line really confused them all. They felt it was unbelievable that a twelve or fifteen-pound test line could hold a powerful fifty-pound salmon. Not often did a hand-troller, using a much heavier line, land one of that size. Instead of playing the fish they had to pull it in forcefully, usually breaking something or tearing the hook from the inside of the jaw.

We had noticed a skiff with two older men who fished diligently almost every day. They were brothers and one was blind. He did the rowing, directed by his brother who took care of the baiting and lines. When they rowed close one day to watch Stu jig herring, the sighted brother explained every move to the other. Both were delighted when Stu rigged up a spare pole with line and jigging hooks for them.

In the following days we watched with amusement and more than a little satisfaction when the sighted brother pulled up a string of wriggling herring, counting them for the blind fellow who then clapped his hands while both laughed hilariously. Others soon found jigging to be much more productive than the old way. Judging by their uproarious shouts of pleasure and amusement, it was also a source of great sport.

Before long the aloofness disappeared. The natives came eagerly to investigate our gear and ask questions. Stu showed them how to use poles, reels and light nylon line for salmon fishing. Often when we heard a whoop and a holler we would see one of the young men standing in his skiff, his pole bent and reel speedily unwinding with a loud buzz.

While unloading our catch one day, including three kings over fifty pounds, we overheard one swarthy Indian say to another, "Dat little woman, she catch dos beeg slugs, one behindt de odder on dat little tread."

"Did you notice the natives don't leave now when we start fishing?" I asked Stu one day.

"Yes, I feel better, too," he responded. "Maybe they'll invite us to join the tribe," he added in jest.

"Jim and Mary deserve a lot of credit for their tactful understanding and help," I said, gratefully.

Later the owners of the fishing supply stores in Juneau told how they had received messages from the native hand-trollers by radio or letter, saying simply, "Send us gear like Neelys use."

"A white man teaching the Indian how to fish?" one merchant remarked smiling, "that's a switch!"

After a time of profitable fishing, we felt entitled to splurge a bit so sent an order to a Juneau grocery store for a watermelon to be sent out on the weekly mail plane. We were waiting at the ramp when the plane arrived, eagerly looking forward to a luscious treat. The $9.25 combined air-freight charge and the cost of the twelve-pound melon somewhat dampened our anticipation but Stu carried it carefully to the skiff and we hurried back across the channel, determined to keep the melon out of sight and eat it all ourselves. We had just secured the boat on the beach and started for the cabin when we saw the Indian chief and his wife walking towards us along the beach. Having been so intent on getting ashore quickly and up to the cabin we were taken completely by surprise and had no way to hide our costly treat.

There was nothing to do but invite our visitors in as we

certainly didn't want to offend the village chief. Stu cut each a conservative slice of the big melon while our guests exclaimed over the size and pretty red color on the inside. It was a real tasty one.

The Indian couple, both considerably overweight, made no move to leave when they had finished their piece, and it was obvious they didn't intend to leave while there was any left. The only fresh fruit they had access to was the local wild berries. They held on to their empty tin plates and eyed the remainder of the melon on the table. My hungry fisherman glanced at me and with a "I give up" shrug of his shoulders, he cut the rest of it into four large portions.

As she finished the last bite, the old squaw wiped her mouth on her sleeve and said, "Dem beeg berries are de best kind."

12

Neighbors in the North

Autumn brought storms and heavy rains. Flocks of migrating ducks and geese passed overhead. Before going on southward, many stayed for an indefinite time in Mitchell Bay and the tidal flats at the head of the Inlet. The height of the social life we were to experience in Angoon was our contact with the natives at gatherings on the fish-buyer's boat.

One reason for this was the inconvenience in getting to the community's center of activity. After crossing Kootznahoo Inlet we had to walk the half mile from the plane float. I was ever aware of bear lurking in the brush and was afraid of the many hungry-looking dogs. Or we could climb from our boat onto a worn wooden ladder scaling the perpendicular rock cliff directly in front of the store. I tried it once. After one glance into the dark green water, fathoms deep below me, I kept my eye on the next rung, not even watching for the top rung which it seemed I would never reach. When we were ready to go home, I took one look over the edge into the murky water twenty feet below and announced bluntly, "I'm going to walk back to the plane float." There was a small bight on the opposite side of the peninsula where the natives could beach their small craft near their homes, but for us it meant going around Danger Point, the rocky reef jutting into Chatham Straits. It was several miles farther and there was always the possibility of being stranded in rough weather. So we rarely went to the village and not at all after dark.

"I haven't seen any bars in town," I commented one day. "But I have seen some natives drinking and a few pretty drunk."

"Most of the native villages are dry," Stu said. "It's against the law to sell liquor here but there's always some boot-legging going on, and someone will always sneak a bottle in for a price."

Thanks to Jim and Mary, our relationship with the fishermen was now agreeable and mutually respectful, and considering the travel difficulties we could see no reason for any further contact.

"That's good enough," Stu declared, "I'm satisfied with the way it is now."

The fishing season ended and we moved into a cabin less than a half mile farther up the beach which we rented from a fisherman who was going to Sitka for the winter. In the spring and summer he would live on his boat. Although the cabin had only one large room and a small storage room, it was sturdily built with double walls, porch and a good foundation. Even the outhouse had no drafty cracks in the walls. The kitchen range was sufficient for both cooking and heating. The large oven, when open, would lessen the shivering of hurried baths in the wash tub. Sparkling clear water was piped from a spring on the hillside behind the cabin to an outside barrel until freezing weather presented problems.

A small bight in the shoreline formed a tiny natural harbor in front of the cabin and safe moorage at the sturdy, well-anchored float. Our only neighbor lived about 300 yards down the beach.

"Do you think it will be too lonesome for you here?" Stu asked as I stood watching a little old man cutting driftwood on the beach.

"I don't think so," I replied slowly. "But I do wish that old fellow there had a wife so I'd have one woman to gossip with."

"They call him 'Old John'. Let's go over and get acquainted," Stu suggested.

Old John was as much a part of Alaska as the rugged wilderness surrounding his one-room cabin on the rocky shore of Kootznahoo Inlet. He was a small lean man, slightly stooped but alert, grimy from the top of his sagging hat to his well-worn boots. It was quite obvious that neither he nor his clothes were familiar with soap and water. Piercing blue eyes dominated a face well-etched by eighty-nine years of living.

The beach in front of Old John's place had a wide gradual slope, strewn with harsh boulders partially covered with seaweed and kelp. At extremely high tide the water reached within a few feet of the sturdy unpainted cabin where he lived with his eight cats. A small clearing separated his cabin from the dense woods which covered most of the island.

"Here," he gestured with a wave of his arm, "I grow

95

potatoes and rutabagas. That's all I need." Then he added, "I plant the rutabagas closest to the house and when the deer come to eat the tops I can shoot one from the window. Don't have so far to drag it that way."

"Sounds like a good deal," Stu acknowledged.

"But I can't see as good as I used to and sometimes I miss, then me and the cats don't have any meat," Old John went on, shaking his head sadly.

"I'll rustle venison for you while I'm here, John," Stu assured him.

Late in the fall Old John would send an order to Sitka with a fisherman friend for his winter supplies, which consisted of two slabs of bacon and two eighty-pound sacks of rolled oats. My grocery list was less simple. After much mulling over how much flour, sugar, coffee and other items we would need for the winter, I was finally ready to give the list to the fishbuyer on his last trip to Juneau. For fresh meat we would have to depend on hunting for deer, ducks and geese. Occasionally a fisherman would be stopping by to tie to our dock for the night or to wait out a storm and would be glad to bring us anything we needed from town on his return trip. Mostly we looked forward to the latest newspapers and magazines.

Plane service was uncertain in the winter and sometimes in stormy weather there was no mail for weeks. The couple who lived by the plane float held our mail for us so we seldom had to go to the village post office.

Old John either didn't remember or was reluctant to talk about when he came to Angoon and from where. No one we talked with knew when he had built his cabin and settled there.

"Guess he's just always been here," was the general opinion.

We were told that Old John was the first depositor in B.M. Behrends Bank in Juneau sometime in the 1880's. Years earlier he had spent months prospecting for gold. Talking about his diggings, even sparingly, kindled a new gleam in his eyes, now growing dim, and a note of excitement mixed with wistfulness would creep into his voice.

"There's still some there too," he ended.

"Is it far from here?" Stu probed casually.

"No, but it's hard to find," the wary old fellow said and changed the subject.

Long before we knew him, Old John had married an Indian and lived with her until her death.

"She was a mean old woman," he confided to Stu, "but she sure could cook sea lion."

96

Sea lions are difficult to kill; even after scoring a hit with a rifle, the trick is to get to it before it sinks. Like the hair seal, it is much desired by the natives for food. Both mammals have a strong fishy flavor, however seal liver is mild and tasty, not at all fishy. We have eaten it many times and prefer it to either beef or venison liver.

I tried to hide my concern at the prospect of accidents or sickness a hundred miles from a hospital or doctor. Luckily we were both healthy and never suffered any mishaps that required anything more than a few bandaids. A government nurse visited the school in Angoon once a month and could always be depended on by others for advice or help in an emergency.

There were many instances of risky rescue flights to bring an accident victim or gravely ill person to the hospital. Sometimes it was necessary to take the doctor out to a patient in an isolated home or boat. The much admired bush pilots were often called in in the middle of the night or in frightful weather.

Neighbors in Alaska are great—even when at some distance, anyone, whether acquainted or not, will investigate if something seems to be amiss. In the winter the absence of smoke from a chimney or light from a window can be reason for concern, as well as the failure to see usual activity such as wood chopping and other chores.

One day Old John took sick. After several days, as he became steadily worse, a friend of his who happened by, contacted other friends in the village and they all agreed that the storekeeper should radio for a plane. In spite of his protests that he could take care of himself, he was put aboard and taken to the hospital in Sitka. In less than two weeks he was home, indignant but seemingly recovered. When Stu went over to see him, he complained. "They damn near killed me. They gave me a bath and my hair turned white overnight."

He had a little dinghy. Fishermen usually carry one aboard their trollers to use in emergency or to go to the beach when anchored off-shore. John's was small enough to be easily dragged down the beach to the water. Only eight feet long, it was square across the stern where he sat, facing forward while rowing. With two or three cats watching his every move from the bow, he fished around the kelp patches for sea bass and kelp cod for his cats and halibut, one of the best seafoods, for himself. Once in a while he'd catch a salmon but usually they were farther off shore, too far for him to venture out in such a small skiff.

Old John also used his dinghy to tow in driftwood or logs, anything that could be used for firewood. At high tide he could

97

beach the salvaged wood close to the cabin. One day while attempting to attach a tow line to a log he lost his balance and went over backwards into the icy water. We happened to be home that day and Stu was just bringing in an armload of wood when he suddenly yelled, "Old John's tipped over!" Dropping the wood, he dashed down to our boat moored at the float, just as a troller heading in towards the harbor saw the old fellow's predicament. Luckily he was close enough to help and within a few minutes had maneuvered his boat alongside the log the old man was hanging on to and pulled him out of the water.

After the fisherman had tied up to the dock both he and Stu urged Old John to get out of his cold soaked clothes, offering him dry ones to wear home.

He refused, saying, "What the hell you fussing about? Got a good fire going at home, I'll dry out." And with that he plodded down the beach, water sloshing in his boots and dripping off his clothes.

"Poor Old John," I thought, "this is the second time this year he's had an unintentional bath."

Late that evening Stu went over to see if he was all right. He had not removed any of his clothes except his boots. He wore bib overalls, wool shirt, and the heavy wool underwear worn year around by most Alaskan fishermen. Sitting close to the red hot stove, little pools of water formed on the bare floor as it dripped from those heavy clothes. Concerned that the frail-looking old fellow would catch pneumonia, Stu looked in on him again the next morning. He came back shaking his head.

"He's a tough old fellow," Stu said. "He was cooking breakfast still wearing the same clothes. They looked mostly dry except for the thick places like the cuffs and pockets. I asked him how he was doing. 'Never mind me, I'm all right,' he grumbled."

"I guess he figures he's gotten along all these years the way he is," I surmised, "and he needs no interference now."

Late in the fall we hunted ducks and geese in Mitchell Bay, or rather I went along while Stu hunted. Although I knew how to use a rifle, I never did like a shotgun and had no desire to own one. Here and there splashes of golden leaves contrasted with the usual lush green of the rain forests. Even the slightest breeze started the bright leaves fluttering to the ground. Soon the willows and alders would be bare.

"Get down and keep quiet," Stu warned me over and over when he tried to get a shot at low-flying birds. I didn't mind him shooting the ducks but I confess I often hoped he would miss the beautiful geese. I had always loved to hear and watch the graceful majestic birds in their V formation, until they disappeared from sight.

I suppose the honking of wild geese means something different to everyone . . . to some a juicy roast. I'll admit a well-prepared goose makes a mighty tasty meal, a delightful change from our diet of venison and fish. But to me the chorus of vibrant and persistent cries carry a note of plaintive entreaty — as if searching — for what? I am thrilled and sad at once.

Early in the winter we canned venison using my indispensable pressure cooker, and smoked sausage in bags I hand-sewed from oatmeal sacks. Stu rubbed the hindquarters with salt and pepper and after leaving it to drain twenty-four hours, he smoked the hams slowly for several days and nights. I believe his favorite winter pastime was experimenting with different methods of preserving venison.

He cut thin strips of meat, one to one and a half inches wide and ten or twelve inches long, rubbed them well with salt and coarse pepper, then let them hang until they had dripped dry. He preferred not soaking the meat in a brine as some people do. Jerky is usually cured by drying only, but we did not have a proper place to dry a large amount so it was hung in the smoke house for weeks, with just enough heat to promote drying and give a mild smoky flavor. I have never tasted jerky that equalled Stu's "pride and joy." I was tempted to nibble at it constantly.

A gradual chill swept over the land as the winter shadows lengthened. Soon a blanket of snow covered everything changing the predominant greens to sparkling white except for the changing hues of the sea water. The winter was half gone already. What happened to all those empty hours I had expected to find hard to fill? Trying to make meals appealing with a limited variety of food took time, as did baking bread and concocting a goody once in a while. I missed fresh vegetables most of all. Old John shared a couple of rutabagas with us occasionally and although he accepted whatever tid-bit I offered him, he made it plain he was self-sufficient.

"Wash-day today," I announced twice a week after breakfast.

"I'll have to pour hot water over the faucet first," Stu sometimes replied, "and break the ice in the barrel." Although the pipe to the spring was buried underground sometimes the water froze at the spring. After heating the water in a washtub on the stove, I used a generous portion of soap and soaked the clothes two or three hours. Then with a minimum of rubbing on the washboard and more rinsing I called it good enough.

I draped a few pieces at a time over lines strung at the back of the stove, which made it seem like the lines were never empty. On clear or windy days I hung the wash outside, where they froze dry in cold weather.

"Come look, quick!" I exclaimed one evening, holding the door to the porch ajar a few inches. Stu reached my side just in time to see a pair of shining green eyes disappear in the darkness. "What are they?" I asked. "There were three of them when I opened the door."

"Those rascals are martens," he replied, "belong to the same family as mink, otter and your favorite, the weasel. Their fur is valuable, too."

The freezing weather now allowed us to hang a skinned deer carcass on one end of the porch that was enclosed with a strong wire net. The fresh meat attracted the creatures, about two feet long with short legs and lustrous brown fur. I often watched for the glittering green eyes, like bright gems in the reflection of the lamp light. In the mornings the snow around the cabin was patterned with tiny tracks which led to the woods and to the discarded bones and scraps of venison.

The weather moderated early in the spring bringing heavy rains, and leaving books still unread, socks undarned, and letters unwritten, dissipating the delusion that northern winters held plenty of leisure hours. I had mixed feelings. I loved winter-time with its soft touch of snow on my cheeks and the stimulating tramps through the fluffy mass to follow the tracks of the creatures of the wilderness. I loved the nights, with the moon and stars larger and more brilliant than anyone could imagine, and the cozy comfort of long evenings beside a fragrant wood fire.

And yet I welcomed the fresh breezes and warmer rains of springtime. I could hang the washing out without bundling up in warm coats. The days grew longer and I sat in the sun. Boats came up the inlet more often and a few stopped at our float; sometimes, to my delight, there would be a woman aboard. I looked forward eagerly to the bustle of the coming fishing season, the return of the fishbuyer's boat and especially to mingling with people again.

Making a living was the uppermost consideration now and I was content and happy to take my place beside my husband in whatever he chose to do but I still quietly cherished the now dormant yearning to journey even farther north and seek out distant and to me unknown regions.

13

Tyee

We were all set to start fishing when we learned that Jim and Mary would not be back to buy salmon. Jim had unexpectedly had an attractive offer to hire out with his boat and felt he could not turn it down. Because many of the trolling boats carried ice and sold their catch in town, Jim's dependence on the hand-trollers and other small boats was not sufficiently profitable to maintain his sixty-foot vessel, home and family.

A friendly fisherman had already frozen a few big salmon for us that he had watched us catch inside the bay near our cabin, but he was ready to move on and the rumor that another fish buyer would come in once a week was too uncertain to depend on. Besides we had no ice to keep salmon that long. We were both disappointed and frustrated because it was clear that another move was necessary.

"Why don't you go to Tyee?" the fisherman asked. "It's really a better place for a small boat than here. There's a cold storage and you won't have these mean tidal currents in this channel to contend with."

"Is there a place to live?" I asked hopefully.

"There's a cannery there and some cabins," he replied, "a company store too. Of course it all closes down after fishing season is over."

Stu helped the troller to cast off and get under way then turned to look at me with a mixture of uncertainty and expectancy.

"What do you think about it, shall we go?" he asked.

"Sounds good to me," I answered with enthusiasm and I think, to his surprise. "Let's go see. Maybe there'll even be ice cream in the store."

So three days later, in the spring of 1952, I again packed up our belongings, including thirty cans of venison and what remained of our dwindling grocery supply, and we glided out of the bay early in the afternoon with one last look at the snug little cabin in its wilderness setting. There would be memories, but whatever regrets I might have felt were already being crowded out by the anticipation of a new venture.

Tyee was perhaps forty miles farther south, on the very tip of Admiralty Island. Here and there the pale green of the new leaves on alders and willows broke the solid deeper green of the forest above the rocky shoreline.

With only a few more miles to go, a nasty squall from the north overtook us and soon rough waves forced us to slow down. I glanced anxiously from the mounting white water to the rocky shore. We had been warned of the bad rip-tides around Point Gardner, only a few miles from Tyee, and as we neared the point Stu released the throttle still more while he stood to look ahead.

"Too rough. We can't make it around the point," he shouted above the noisy motor.

Facing him in the sixteen-foot skiff, I turned to look where not far ahead the Point Gardner light stood guard over angry frothing seas.

"The rip-tide is bad. We'll go back a ways and find a hole in the shoreline somewhere and crawl in a while," Stu said.

After we pitched and bucked twenty minutes more, Stu found a tiny sheltered bight and eased the craft in slowly while I lay flattened on the bow watching for rocks. With the boat secure on a few feet of sandy beach, we went ashore and Stu built a small fire. Several times he walked around rocks to where he could see the point only to report it was still too rough to travel. Finally as twilight began to close in and we could still see the spray from waves crashing on the rocky beach, we knew we could never make it to Tyee before dark.

"It's too dangerous to travel after dark even if it calms down," Stu warned. "I'm not familiar with the water and reefs here. See if you can find us a bite to eat, then I'll fix you a comfortable place to sleep and we'll leave at daybreak." I smiled at this attempt to console me. I knew he wasn't disappointed; he enjoyed nothing better than to spend a night by a camp fire, and although stormy, it wasn't raining.

He built a larger fire at the open end of a triangle formed by two large drift logs crossing at a right angle. Scooping away gravel and debris, he spread a sleeping bag alongside each log with the fire at our feet. There was no sign of anxiety on his ruddy face, only an unruffled confidence which soon rubbed off on me.

"I'll sit by the fire a couple hours to watch the boat and retie it when the tide changes," he said, his large strong hands outstretched to the blaze.

"I'm not sleepy yet so I'll sit with you a while," I responded. The scent of the smoke was pleasurable, the festive crackling of the fire fascinating to watch. An owl hooted back in the woods. The waters had calmed and we heard whales spouting.

"What about bear?" I asked apprehensively, glancing into the dark shadows behind me.

"No danger with a big fire going," he assured me, throwing another piece of driftwood on the fire.

Becoming drowsy I crawled into my sleeping bag. Gazing overhead I was sure there were more stars in the sky than I had ever seen before and never had they seemed so near.

Unusual but not unpleasant, I mused to myself, succumbing to the tranquility of the now quiet night and the age-old comfort of a primitive camp fire.

I shifted to avoid a large pebble under one shoulder. My mind went back over the chain of circumstances that led to sharing my life with this quiet man who belonged to the outdoors; to traveling in this wilderness over these unpredictable waters; nights with only the stars above us. Never had my wildest dreams included all this although I had little idea of what was ahead when my sister and I took off for Alaska on a small freighter and a shoestring budget.

"It's daylight and we can travel," I heard Stu say, shaking my shoulder vigorously. It seemed I had just closed my eyes. Soon we were under way once more.

Tyee, an Indian word meaning "Big Fish," was a well-sheltered deep-water harbor in Murder cove, with a fresh-water creek emptying into it at the head of the cove. The unattractive name of the cove was in stark contrast to the beauty and charm of the mile-long inlet with its evergreen, heavily-wooded shores lined with beach grass. In the 1860's, shortly after Russia sold Alaska to the United States, Tlingit Indians, claiming this as their territory, murdered some white prospectors here, and the name Murder Cove survived.

The cannery that had operated here for many years was clustered together with a mess hall, bunk house, cold storage and other buildings, on both sides of a plank walk-way on the south shore of the harbor. As we pulled up to a long and narrow floating dock, I counted fourteen small, look-alike, barn-red cabins spaced along the far end of the boardwalk, which was just above the high-tide line. Only the first one seemed to be occupied.

"Let's go find the cannery superintendent right away and ask about a place to live," Stu said as we climbed the wooden terraced ramp to the floor level of the big dock and other buildings.

Mike Goodman greeted us with a friendly smile and hearty handshake, then invited us to the mess hall for coffee.

"The cabins are for the native women who come over from Kake to work on the piecing table. We have a crew of white men and a crew of Filipinos will be coming later. You can have a cabin rent-free if the Missus here will work in the cannery when needed. Some days it may be only a couple hours, other times maybe all day or over-time."

"Looks like this is up to you," Stu said, looking at me dubiously.

"You can take your pick of the cabins," Mike added, "and there is nothing else here to live in."

"I think it's a deal," I said. This looked good to me, at least I knew where I'd be sleeping tonight. There was a store and electric lights and people. Also, I had never worked in a cannery before; it might be an interesting experience. It would certainly be different.

I picked a two-room roughly-finished cabin next to the one occupied by George and Frances Pierce, a young couple who worked for the company, with George also acting as winter watchman. After applying buckets of soapy water to the floor with a stiff broom, I washed the front window that looked out on the water and the two tiny bedroom windows, while Stu replaced rusted lengths of stove chimney with new ones from the store. I rounded up empty orange crates to substitute for cupboards and shelves. Our clothes were hung on nails on the walls. The furniture consisted of a comfortable looking bed, small cast iron stove, a table and two chairs. Stu found an old sink out in the brush. He cut a hole in the wall and attached a piece of hose to the company water line and we had clear cold water from the creek.

By evening a blazing fire and the fragrant smell of coffee added a touch of warmth and comfort to our new home. I had just set the empty coffee cups in the sink when suddenly the lights flickered off and on twice.

"That's the ten minute warning," Stu told me. "They shut the generator off at ten every night, so get to bed; we're going fishing in the morning."

After a few days Stu was ecstatic.

"There's miles and miles of herring out there, more than I've ever seen, and good fishing on the flats out of the way of the big trollers, and there's big kelp patches. It's so handy to sell at the cold storage and we can even come in for lunch."

I snickered a little at the last remark, knowing how often lunches had been postponed when fishing.

The 'flats' was a large area of fairly shallow water from eight to thirty fathoms deep beyond which flowed Chatham Straits with depths up to 100 fathoms or more (six feet to a fathom). Large kelp beds grew in the more shallow waters. We soon learned where to fish and when the tide seemed the best.

This area was the feeding grounds of a family of unusually large salmon. Because of the abundance of herring, many of which sought the protection of the kelp beds to avoid their predators, we found that our tempting bait spelled disaster for many a slug (salmon) following herring into the kelp.

One day Stu dropped the anchor in the edge of a kelp bed at one of the 'hot' spots, then let out forty or fifty feet of anchor line until the boat had drifted with the tide and away from the kelp. He secured the line to a buoy in the bow of the boat and then caught a few herring for bait.

"Just look at the herring," I exclaimed, leaning over the edge of the boat. "I've never seen them so thick."

"It's a heck of a big school," he said.

"How do you know how big it is?" I asked.

"Look how far out the sea gulls and eagles are circling and diving. . . .Got a strike!" he suddenly shouted, "Throw the buoy over." I reeled in my line, threw the buoy over and started the motor. With our light lines it was impossible to pull a big salmon against the strong tide, so we followed it slowly while carefully playing the frantic fish as it circled or sounded.

We had landed several over forty pounds and were again returning to the buoy when we saw the big backs of two whales break water right where we had been fishing.

"I'm not going to argue with them," Stu said, slowing the boat. "We'll wait until they move on."

"Do whales chase the salmon?" I asked.

"No, they feed on small sealife like herring and plankton. Actually, whales in the vicinity are sometimes a sign of good salmon fishing. The big monsters cripple and stun lots of herring with their powerful tails as they go through a school, then the salmon follow and pick up the cripples."

"And we pick up the salmon, huh?" I finished.

"There are eighteen eagles perched on Point Gardener Rock

105

— I counted them," I said, somewhat smugly, not to be outdone by his own observations, "and a lot of fishducks."

"You're supposed to be paying attention to your fishing." Stu had once again anchored the boat. "We seem to have a lot of competition from the 'locals' today," he joked as he turned to me and grinned. With fishing like this, who wouldn't be in a good humor?

A little later a mother and baby seal poked their heads out of water and looked at us curiously.

"The seals won't bother the fishing," Stu said as we watched them. "But I don't like the sea lions, they're nasty. They scare the salmon away and they'll take one right off your line, too."

An hour later he suggested we take a run out to see how far the herring school extended. "The tide's changing and the salmon have quit biting."

"I'm ready to go home, too," I added.

We went north about a mile to Point Gardner. Approaching slowly we watched the bald eagles swooping down over the water, sometimes rising with a herring in clenched talons but often empty-clawed. Going a mile or more out into Chatham Straits we turned south, all the while running through herring so thick it appeared as a dark cloud on the water. When Stu shut off the motor the flipping of the large school as it fed on shrimp spawn or other feed floating on the surface of the water sounded like a steady fall of raindrops and could be heard for some distance.

As we continued on several miles toward Yasha Island, porpoises raced us on both sides of the boat and when we saw sea lions near the island we turned towards home. Never were we out of sight of the herring, a seemingly endless supply in spite of the many predators preying upon them.

There were thirty or forty boats, both trollers and seiners, tied to the docks when we pulled in to sell our day's catch. The fishermen from Kake had brought their women over and were busy carrying their luggage to the cabins. Boxes, duffle bags, piles of bedding and wash tubs full of household goods were piled along the boardwalk.

"Seining season opens tomorrow," Mike told us when we unloaded 164 pounds of gutted red king salmon. There were no whites. "The cannery will start up the next day," he continued, handing Stu nearly eighty dollars in cash. "Be ready to go to work when the whistle blows, Virginia."

I just had time to apply a can of white kalsomine to the walls, put down a roll of cheap linoleum and hang brightly checked curtains, both from a mail order house, making our cabin the envy of cannery row.

14

The Cannery

Our quiet little harbor had come alive. Boats of all descriptions glided in and out until far into the night, those with salmon aboard lining up at the loading dock. Workers hurried between bunk-houses, the cookhouse and cannery buildings, accompanied by shouts, laughter and the clanking of machinery. The boardwalk along cannery row creaked under the weight of the increased traffic.

In the evenings, native girls dressed in many-hued ruffled dresses from the mail order house, strolled from one end of the boardwalk to the other. Children played on the beach in front of the cabins, the older ones trying to keep the toddlers from straying. I noticed the children were quick to offer to go to the store for a loaf of bread or other small items and usually returned munching on a candy bar.

"You'll have to fish alone today," I said while dishing up bacon and eggs. "The cannery is starting to operate this morning."

"I know," Stu replied, "but I'll be in to eat lunch with you."

I was getting acquainted with the wife of the skipper of one of the cannery boats when the eight o'clock whistle blew. We were both handed white cotton gloves and assigned to the piecing table with two other women, two on each side. A Filipino crew operated the 'iron chink' which gutted and cut off the heads of four species of salmon, all smaller than the kings. The silvery-sided kings, the choicest of the species, were mild-cured, being much too expensive for the canned salmon market. They were caught mainly by trolling boats and gutted as soon as possible. Because they spawned early in the spring long before the season opened for seine fishing and fishtraps, the kings were not schooled up at the same time as the canning species.

Next, native women, working at a sliming table with running water, scraped out the blood and slime. The fish were then cut into uniform sizes and packed into cans, all by machinery. The filled cans then went to the piecing table on a moving belt. Ours was the final check, watching for scraps of bone or skin hanging over the side and checking for underweight cans which we remedied by adding a small chunk of salmon from a panful near at hand. We became quite adept at detecting a light weight can just by lifting it when a piece only a half-inch square was needed to bring it up to the required weight. From the piecing table the cans moved on to the vacuum sealer and finally into the huge pressure cookers, known as retorts.

Expert splitters, that process a trade in itself, split the kings deftly along each side of the backbone. The slabs were then carefully cleaned under running water and salted down in huge barrels called tierces which held 800 pounds each. After soaking for a period of time in the brine, the mild-cured salmon were shipped to markets mainly in the big cities on the east coast where they were smoked like slabs of bacon.

Cannery tenders plied the waters buying salmon from seine boats that used nets to encircle schools of fish. Each cannery had several fishtraps located at selected points close to the shoreline. One morning sitting on the washbench outside the door of our cabin, I watched the crew of the rigging scow, a motorized heavy work boat, assembling one of the traps. The large enclosure formed by floating logs that were cabled together was then towed out and secured in place with huge anchors weighing nearly a ton. A funnel-like series of wire net enclosures were then hung from the logs in such a manner as to divert traveling schools of salmon into an opening in the trap. When hundreds of salmon had been trapped the opening would be closed and the fish brailled into the cannery fish scow. The two trap watchmen who lived in a tiny shack were sometimes tempted to enhance their personal income by selling a few hundred to prowling fish pirates in the dark of the night. To try and thwart the temptation, each year different watchmen, preferably strangers to each other, were assigned to the traps by the cannery superintendent.

Because salmon on the way to their spawning streams always traveled in schools and followed the shoreline, the fish-traps were extremely efficient and possibly contributed more to the ravage of the salmon population than any other one cause. Since working in the cannery was a new experience for me, I listened with interest to what anyone and everyone had to say about this facet of the fishing industry.

The majority of the canneries and traps have been owned and operated for over half a century by big companies on the east and west coasts of the United States and these companies have done nothing to conserve the salmon runs. In the twenty years prior to our arrival at Tyee cannery production had dropped more than seventy-five per cent. In recent years there had been some attempt by a federal commission to regulate the number of hours and days fishing was permitted, but it was a much belated attempt.

There were good years or specific areas in which there were big runs of either silvers, pinks, chums or sock-eyes — the four species that were canned. But the over-all picture was not encouraging as the boats came in less than loaded and the cannery hours diminished. Old-timers shook their heads and spoke of the days when the salmon schools were so dense at spawning time that one could walk across the channels on the backs of the salmon.

There were many days when the cannery work was finished by noon and I could fish with Stu in the afternoon and evening. Although the summer days were long often the fishing was so brisk on an evening tide we ignored the time until long after sundown. Reluctant to leave we continued fishing until it was so dark we couldn't see which direction the hooked salmon was taking the line; only the glow from the phosphorus in the water revealed the whereabouts of the king as it thrashed about.

Sometimes after a twelve or fourteen-hour day I was too tired to cook and we ate cold sandwiches or whatever was handy, and after several such days we ignored the clock in the morning and slept until noon. There were bad days when we sat in a steady rain for hours, my hands so cold I could hardly cut a bait. Tired and cranky I could easily find something to complain about.

"What's that awful smell?" I grumbled.

"I think a couple herring got stuck under the floor boards and they get over-ripe pretty quick," Stu explained quietly.

"Well, it stinks," I retorted, wondering why the offensive smells that at times upset me, didn't seem to bother him at all.

"I'll wash it out good tonight," he said, a bit of impatience in his voice. Then added, "I think it's time to quit for the day."

"Can't now," I blurted, forgetting my gripes as I grabbed my pole. "I've got one on."

During ten days of perfect weather in August we thought we had hit the jack-pot when we averaged over $100. a day.

Sometimes after we had landed a big king I would hurry and bait up while Stu motored the boat back to pick up the buoy. I just loved to quickly slip my bait in the water while he was retying the boat to the buoy can; with good luck I occasionally hooked another salmon before he finished, then I smugly shouted, "Come on! Let's get going. What are you waiting for?"

"It was a lucky day for us when we came to Tyee," Stu declared late one afternoon. "I never dreamed of such good fishing with rod and reel like we've had around the kelp beds."

"And I never realized there were so many big kings, or that they followed the herring into the kelp like this. It's too bad the trollers can't fish here," I replied.

"It's a good thing for us they can't. It's too shallow for them. They'd hang up their gear on the bottom. Besides, they need to work bigger areas. They have a big overhead and have to land lots of salmon to make it pay. Looks like we can go Outside this fall," he netted another big king and dumped it flopping on the floorboards. Stu put down the new fiberglass pole that had by now replaced the old bamboo ones, tapped the fish on the head with a small club then covered it with a wet gunny sack alongside ten others. Two would run over sixty pounds, four over fifty and none under forty. All were red except one.

With our simple way of life and a minimum of expenses, stemming mostly from the lack of any place to spend money, we figured our income would suffice until the next season.

"Wait until we go south and I get to go shopping," I warned. "Let's pull anchor and go in. I think they've quit biting and I'm getting tired and hungry anyway."

Even as I walked up to the cabin to start supper while Stu gutted the salmon on the beach a swarm of vicious no-see-ums, tiny black gnat-like insects, encircled my head. The savage little beasts about the size of fleas attack any uncovered part of one's body, inflicting painful bites or stings that cause the skin to become swollen and irritated. They will get into the eyes, nose, and mouth if open, and as far into the hair or under a hat as possible. Insect repellent is only partially helpful and is messy as the no-see-ums stick to the oily lotion. Luckily, they will not go inside a building even with the door wide open but swarm along the beaches and over the muskegs. Even a slight breeze will blow them away and they disappear when it rains. The tiny pests won't go out over the water very far from shore or fishing would become unbearable.

I had just entered the door when Stu began to holler.

"Bring something down and keep these damn bugs away

from my face," he sputtered, flinging his arms right and left.

I grabbed a dish towel in each hand and by waving them violently and continuously, I managed to keep the pests away from his face and mine until he had finished with the cleaning. It had turned cloudy and the air was quiet — perfect conditions for the bloodthirsty little predators. Almost before we left the beach, greedy seagulls and ravens croaking and screeching at each other, had cleaned up the left-overs.

Stu splashed cold water on his face and neck. "I'm going to make a cleaning trough I can attach to the boat so I can clean the salmon before coming in." He rinsed his mouth too. "I'm sick and tired of fighting those blasted things."

Later that evening it started to rain and the wind came from the southwest.

"Looks like it might be stormy tomorrow," he said. "If it is, I'll get some kippered salmon going in the smokehouse. I put a big one aside in the cold storage."

"Good," I smacked my lips. "I can almost taste it now!"

15

Beachcombing

I distinctly remember the delectable smoky whiffs from Stu's smokehouse a short distance behind our shanty. He made the best kippered salmon I have ever eaten. Using only large kings, preferably over thirty pounds, he cleaned each thoroughly, cut it into chunks four or five inches square and carefully salted each piece with a large salt shaker. He never soaked the salmon in brine as sometimes recommended, but preferred to place the salted chunks, skin side down, on the stiff wire racks called hardware cloth. They were left there to drip overnight or at least twelve hours without any heat or smoke. By morning the draining had stopped and the meat had firmed up. One of the important benefits of the waiting period was that the skin would not stick to the rack during or after the smoking was finished.

He started the smoking with a very slow fire using alder wood which he had cut in a slough at the upper end of Murder Cove soon after we came to Tyee. When possible he used dry wood convinced that green wood left a slightly bitter taste. Many types of pitchless hardwood were used, the kind usually determined by what was available at the time and place. In Angoon he had found both black maple and alder, but at Tyee only alder.

During the first hours of the eighteen to twenty-four hour smoking process, he kept a close watch so as not to cause the salmon to crack or ooze juice from too much heat — but I mustn't reveal all of his secrets. It's sufficient to say that the product of his meticulous process was golden brown squares of thick, luscious, juicy kippered salmon; his pride and joy and rightly so. The tantalizing aroma drifting from the smokehouse brought many seemingly casual drop-ins down the boardwalk to loiter and visit at our cabin.

"I've got to do something noteworthy around here too," I announced one day munching on a hunk of kippered salmon while out fishing. We were anchored on the edge of a two or three-acre kelp patch, the water quiet and so clear I leaned over the edge of the boat to see some of the fascinating sea-life. There were jellyfish of all sizes. Tiny white lacey ones that looked like snowflakes, all pulsating regularly as they floated with the tide. The large ones were transparent slimy masses with long trailing tenacles that reached out to entrap food from the rich nutrient-laden waters. In the midst of these quivering and repelling sea animals were tiny fingerlings, seeking protection from larger fish. Most sea-life shy away from the jellyfish and they are also an annoyance to fishermen when the sticky slimy mess adheres to the lines and bait.

"How deep is it here?" I asked. "I can see those big orange colored, mushroom-shaped anemones on the bottom."

"I think it must be thirty or forty feet," Stu answered. Then added, "I just recently read about these strange and colorful anemones. They are described as primitive multicellular animals and thrive by extending tiny harpoon-like tentacles to poison minute creatures."

"What a mouthful!" I exclaimed. "How did you remember it all?"

Leaning over I picked up one of the kelp bulbs with long ribbon-like streamers floating on the surface of the water and tried to pull loose the long rope-like tube attached to a rock on the bottom. It stuck fast.

"I know what I'll do," I suddenly blurted out. "I'll cut off some of the biggest kelp bulbs, take them in and make a batch of pickles."

"Pickles from kelp? Sounds terrible," came the skeptical response.

"Sure," I assured him. "One of the women at Angoon gave me the recipe but I've never tried it." Stu made a face.

At the first opportunity, I asked the pilot of the mail plane to bring me a bottle of oil of cloves and some cinnamon bark on the next trip. Watching as he wrote my items in his notebook, I wondered if these patient men who willingly rendered so many services beyond their duties, ever received the credit they deserved. With bits of thread or pieces of material they have matched the colors to spools of thread so a dress or quilt could be finished. Or they might be asked to bring anything from cough medicine to a can of snuff to an isolated inhabitant of cabin or fishing boat. More than once we handed a pilot, who we knew only as "Quint", an envelope containing several hundred dollars in currency and asked him to deposit it to our account in the bank.

While waiting for the spices I gathered a bucket full of kelp bulbs and as soon as the pilot smilingly handed me my package I started on my project. In return I promised him a taste. After cutting the thick walls of the hollow bulbs into small chunks, I soaked them in fresh water overnight instead of in brine as would be done with watermelon rind pickles. Then I drained off the water and cooked the kelp in more fresh water until almost tender. Again draining off the water, I covered the cubes with a syrup made of sugar, vinegar and spices and simmered the concoction until the kelp was tender and as transparent looking as its brownish color would allow. I can't say the finished product was as good as real watermelon rind pickles; the mild flavor was mostly of vinegar and spices. Anyway, Stu had to admit it was a tasty substitute served with roast venison when a hundred miles from a grocery store.

Although there were many days of routine part-time work in the cannery, tiresome hours of fishing, non-exciting cooking and housework, never did I get bored. There was always more to do than I had time for, watching the eagles, walking the beaches or exploring creeks and coves and reading. It seemed there was a variety of experiences and exciting observations that kept us alert and life interesting. Like one afternoon as we were coming in from fishing, Stu released pressure on the throttle as we approached the float in front of our cabin and motioned for me to look over the side.

"Now look down in the water and watch closely," he said mysteriously. With the slowed-down prop making less turbulence in the water the boat glided in slowly. I leaned over the side, peering down into clear water, so transparent that I could see every rock and pebble on the bottom. Old clam shells and the usual debris were easily distinguishable.

It was difficult to judge distance in the clear water but I knew it to be from ten to twenty feet deep here, gradually decreasing as we moved closer to the float. Suddenly I saw a movement on the bottom.

"All I see is a big crab," I said. "That's nothing new."

"Keep looking," Stu replied. He was leaning over the edge too.

Then to my surprise I saw other crabs coming from all directions until there were at least a dozen, all obviously

114

following the skiff. Astonishing!

"I didn't know crabs had any brains," I exclaimed. "But they sure look like they're following us!"

"Well, I'd say that means they sure know when and where to come to feed," my husband declared.

Every time we brought in salmon or halibut Stu cleaned them on a small table built onto the end of the float, dumping the refuse into the water. At first it must have been the scent of the blood and guts that attracted the crabs. After a while they must have associated the sound of the motor or sight of the boat or both with a free handout. They came, small and large, as fast as their four pairs of legs could carry them.

We often speared a couple from the boat or float when we felt the urge for a crab feed. Sometimes during an extreme low-tide crabs buried themselves in the sand at the head of the inlet. There were tiny mounds scattered all over and we had only to nudge a crab out with the toe of our boots until we had as many as we wanted. A meal of fresh cracked crab, mayonnaise, crackers and wild asparagus salad was both delicious and satisfying.

In Alaska, beachcomber is a word often applied to someone who lives along the water and rustles much of his food from natural resources, particularly from the sea. During the years we spent in Tyee, seafood from the icy waters of Chatham Straits provided us with a major part of our meat. From spring until late fall some type of salmon was usually available, along with halibut, trout, bass, cod and red snapper. Salmon could be smoked, canned or pickled for the winter. In the wintertime fresh seafoods were not so easily come by, but clams, crabs, sea bass and some cods were usually available.

Although clams, mussels and scallops are in abundance in many parts of southeast Alaska, they are inedible in some areas because of a toxic condition caused by the microflora, *Gonyaulax catenella*.

"We're not going to take any chances, we'll leave them alone while we live out here," Stu told me one day when the subject arose.

"But we ate them in Juneau and Auke Bay," I said.

"I know but there has never been any poison ones found there," he explained. "It must be because it's farther from the main ocean and the red tides don't get in there like out here closer to the ocean."

"Does the red tide cause the poisoning?" I asked.

"You've heard how Peril Straits got its name, haven't you?" he answered my question with another then went on to tell how

115

the narrow passage that divides Chichagof and Baranof Islands derived its ominous name from an incident in the early days when the Russians were exploring Alaska.

"According to the story," he said, "a ship was wrecked on the rocky shore of Peril Straits. Stranded in this remote wilderness, the only food available was mussels. The shipwrecked people all died."

I learned later the microflora, a tiny algael plant, under certain water conditions reproduces at a high rate resulting in a "bloom" or "red tide," the effects of which can last as long as two years. It may appear periodically and last several weeks, most often between May and November. Dose for dose, the paralytic poison is more toxic than strychnine or cyanide. Although the shellfish contain the poison, they are not harmed by it since the toxin is dangerous only to warmblooded animals.

Commercial canning of clams is limited in Alaska and controlled by the Alaska Fish and Game Commission — a government agency which will also advise which areas are free from the toxin where the clams can be eaten freely.

Late summer got me thinking about stocking our larder for the cold season ahead.

"About time to make squaw candy, isn't it?" I asked.

"You're right. I think I'll get a start with those silvers we caught today, there may not be many more." Stu replied.

After thoroughly cleaning and washing the twelve to fourteen-pound salmon, he removed the head and fins, split out the backbone and cut each half into long strips just under two inches wide. I helped by salting the strips and laying them on the racks in the smokehouse where they were smoked slowly for at least a week or until perfectly dry.

Squaw candy is a choice and nutritious food when prepared properly. (I have known of some that could be smelled a half block away.) It makes good snacks and will keep indefinitely. We would often put a piece in our pockets when out in the boat or hunting. Silvers and chums are lean and ideal for dry smoking; kings which are much too fat will crumble and become rancid.

I think most of all we missed fresh vegetables and fruit —well, maybe hot-running water or indoor plumbing came first with me. The lack of some of the comforts of civilization was always the least of my husband's worries. Even during the few months when we had access to the cannery store, there were no fresh vegetables. By the time the mailboat had been on its way for a week, if there was anything fresh left at all it would be in poor condition. And in the winter-time the uncertain schedule was subject to the weather. No matter where we were, if there was a tiny piece of ground at all suitable, Stu, like a magician, would dig a package of radish seed from a coat pocket or a bag of fishing gear.

We did get oranges and apples occasionally if we were willing to pay the price. I remember on one occasion we paid a dollar apiece for three apples. I was aghast, but from the sound of the crunching, my grumbling didn't prevent Stu from enjoying his share to the fullest.

So we found wild plants and berries a reasonable substitute for the unavailable foods. There was goose tongue, a plant with small narrow leaves one to two inches long which we ate raw with a vinegar dressing. Wild cucumber grew two or three feet high and had large leaves which could be eaten green or cooked, but about all I could say for it was that it did have a cucumber flavor.

We liked the wild asparagus best of all. It was a mass of tiny stalks about the size of matches and five to seven inches high. It grew just high enough on the beach so the high tides washed over the wide-spread clumps, leaving a salty tang to the piquant flavored plant when eaten raw as a salad. There was nothing about it that resembled asparagus except the color and shape of the stalks. It was equally good cooked like greens or canned, and added zest to any dinner.

We always gorged on the huge luscious salmonberries, the first fruit of the summer. Heaped over biscuits with sugar and canned milk, it made a delicious shortcake. The berries were too watery and soft for canning but I did can and make jam of wild huckleberries and cranberries. Elderberries made a tasty syrup for hotcakes. The natives put together combinations of salmon eggs and entrails, berries, kelp and seaweed, covered with tallow or seal oil to preserve it and then stored it in kegs. We never got that hungry.

Autumn was hunting time: for venison, to use fresh and to can, or to be made into jerky, and for ducks and geese. At times I welcomed a stormy day when I could relax with a good book.

It was at the end of one such day late in August, with quiet settled over the cannery village, when we suddenly heard the unfamiliar chug-chug or a single cylinder gas-engine boat coming into the harbor. It was quite dark; the days of the brief summer already noticeably shorter. Although we had been about ready to retire for the night, we went out on the porch of our cabin.

"Wonder who's coming in this late in that one-lunger," Stu commented. "Let's walk down to the dock and take a look."

We started down the boardwalk, along with others, who

117

were coming out of their homes and fishing boats as curious as we. The coming of the mailboat or any strange vessel was always a good reason for the inhabitants of the village to gather at the dock. Under the dim lights of the diesel-powered generator, we saw two elderly men on the deck of a small unpainted, very old cabin-boat with an old-timer gas engine.

"Well, I'll be damned!" Stu exclaimed as we drew close enough to see their faces. "That's Old John!"

It *was* our old neighbor from Angoon and a companion, both well into their nineties. They were returning from a summer prospecting for gold. Bearded and clothes worn and dirty, they moved about on the deck of the vessel with a sure and steady step.

"Where you headed for?" Stu asked Old John.

"Pioneers Home in Sitka, I live there now — he does too," he nodded towards his partner. "Come in here for gas," he added.

"Better tie up for the night," Stu and others suggested. But amidst a chorus of "Good Luck!" they cast off, eager to take advantage of the calm weather even though it meant traveling most of the night. Hand in hand my husband and I walked to the far end of the dock and watched until the chugging boat with Old John at the wheel disappeared into the darkness.

16

A King Dethroned

Standing in the open doorway of the cabin on a warm August day, I heard the sound of an outboard motor and a moment later my husband appeared coming around the inlet near the Tyee cannery buildings. Shutting off the throttle, he tipped the motor up free of the water, coasted in to the sandy beach and secured the boat with a long line. As he walked the short distance to the cabin I watched a humming bird hovering over the yellow nasturtiums in my window-box, blooming prolificly in the long daylight hours. It could be late September before a frost put an end to the flowers and Stu's tiny garden patch.

The salmon fishing had tapered off since the first of August so after only three hours work at the cannery I welcomed having the rest of the day free to catch up with a few simple household chores and bake a long promised blueberry pie. I had heated water on the little stove, swept and mopped the floor and put some fishy smelling clothes to soak in the washtub with lots of soap. I had finally smartened up and used stronger soap which cut down on the scrubbing — the clothes might not last as long, I reasoned, but I would.

"Anything out there today?" I questioned with little enthusiasm.

"Mostly halibut," Stu answered. "Want to go down and see a big one?"

"Let's eat lunch first, it's ready," I said. I wasn't interested in seeing just another halibut — not exciting to catch like a salmon, just hard work.

119

Halibut do not run and circle time after time like salmon. They head for the bottom and because of our light lines and limber poles, we have to slowly work them up by hand, keeping pressure on the line all the time. During times when the deep water bottom fish come briefly into more shallow water after herring they can be a time consuming nuisance to strip-fishermen. In this area, the season for halibut was usually closed after June.

"Here's hot water for you," I said, pouring from the tea-kettle into a basin next to the tub of soaking clothes on the wash bench just outside the door.

After a leisurely lunch Stu pushed his chair back, put on his hat and started out the door.

"Come on down and see the monster before I take it over to the cold-storage," he urged.

"All right," I agreed. To myself I thought, 'If it will make him happy, I'll go look at his old halibut.' Following him down the beach to the boat, I leaned over to see the big fish covered with several wet gunny sacks.

"That's not a halibut!" I gasped. It was the wrong shape! A halibut is wide and flat — this was long and thick. I whirled around to see my proud husband watching me with a smug look of satisfaction.

Reaching down he threw back the gunny sacks and there lay the grandaddy of all king salmon! A great silvery beauty!

"How? Where?" I stammered — but here is his own account of the battle for the 73-pound, 10-ounce king as it appeared in the September 1953 issue of *Field and Stream* magazine's annual fishing competition winners, placing second in the Chinook (King) salmon division and currently ranked third in their All Time Top Ten:

The big king was a surprise. In fact, fishing had been slow and I took off alone that morning. My wife, Virginia, who usually not only goes with me but hooks and lands more than her share of big fish, decided to stay in and bake a blueberry pie.

The weather had been warm and dry for Alaska. The water was so clear that the bottom could be plainly seen at 60-feet depth. For this reason, I was fishing very light, using a 15-pound line and a 10-pound 8-foot length leader. I had 1,000 feet of line on the reel and it was lucky I did. The big fish was out 700 or 800 feet several times, and that is getting down on the spool.

Let me try to explain how we fish kings with light tackle in Alaska. We try to anchor the skiff on the edge of a reef or near a kelp bed where the tide flows through the kelp and out over a drop-off into deep water. In other words, the boat is anchored in 60 to 80 feet of water, but you cast your cut bait out, and by the time it settles in the tide it can be in as much as 200 feet of water.

Now the tide here runs three to five miles per hour and in extremes as much as seven. It would be impossible to work a heavy fish against such a current, so when we hook a king we just attach a float to our anchor line, toss it over, and the skiff drifts free. You are soon away from the kelp beds and over deep water where all it takes is a limber pole, plenty of line, time, space, and of course, plenty of that ingredient that stayed with me till the end last August 8 — luck.

But when this 73-pound king hit he didn't run for deep water. He merely bucked up and down a few times then ran up tide and through the edge of a kelp patch. At that time I still wasn't sure that I had hooked a salmon, but I put the reel handle out of gear, laid the pole down in the boat, and ran up (with the motor) to the kelp to free the line.

About this time the reel really started to sing. By the time the line was free of kelp the fish was 500 feet or more out.

About the time I cleared the line and the boat was drifting toward the fish and deep water, he made a beautiful leap. He came out head first. My heart skipped a few beats then. I knew it was my biggest of the year — hooked.

Twice the line fouled in drifting patches of kelp. Several times the line was out uncomfortably close to the end, and once more he jumped — the last time just a few feet from the boat.

After the better part of two of the most anxious, exciting, and happy hours of my life, I slipped the net

over him and heaved him into the boat without a
quiver. I smacked him with a club — then took a
ten-minute break just to look at him and uncramp my
fingers and arms before heading home for that blueberry pie.

17

Going Outside

"It sure is quiet in Murder Cove now," I remarked as we sat at the supper table by the window. Already the sun was dipping behind Baranof Island, leaving a rosy glow on the tips of the snowy peaks.

"This is the way I like it," Stu replied after a long look out of the window. It was the first of October and the cannery crews were gone, the cabins beyond us were empty again and we no longer heard the playing of children on the beach or the giggling girls along the boardwalk. Quiet too, were the electric-light plant, the creaking of machinery, and the cannery whistle.

Only a few boats were left at the float: "Pappy" Short and the Short boys with their trollers, the watchman's little skiff and ours. Ravens on the beach, side-stepping in their peculiar manner, croaked in peaceful communication with each other. The tide lapped gently on the sandy beach — never ceasing. It was a peaceful scene.

"Would you like to go Outside this winter?" Stu asked just as I was silently asking myself whether Alaska had lost its lure as I faced the reality of a stormy winter in this shell of a cabin not built for zero weather.

"Oh yes, I'd like to go," I answered eagerly. My quick answer surprised even myself. Was I really that anxious to go?

"Well, we don't even have to come back, you know," he was saying. "There's nothing to hold us here. All we have is the boat and we can easily sell that."

Not come back? The thought had never occurred to me. I sat silently looking at the water only a few feet from our cabin. Then several streaks of ripples moving toward the beach caught my eyes.

"Look! What's that?" I pointed a finger. A small head popped out of the water, followed by three more. An adult otter and three young ones scampered to the edge of the beach-grass where Stu had weighted down the remains of a small halibut with a rock. I stepped outside to watch and the slinky little creatures stopped their feeding to hiss and glare at me until I went back into the house leaving them to finish their snack undisturbed.

Hesitantly, I started to respond to Stu's suggestion when he interrupted me.

"Can you see something on the other side of the cove?" he asked. I had to strain to see into the deepening shadows.

"Oh, there's a bear," I exclaimed, then in a moment added, "and a deer too."

"Looks like a grizzly, let's see if the deer is afraid of it," Stu said.

Both animals were browsing on beach grass, forty or fifty yards apart. The bear gradually moved closer to the deer and when only a few yards away made a quick movement toward it. The deer leaped swiftly out of reach, running a short distance, then turned to look back, as if teasing the grizzly to try again. After repeating this maneuver twice, the frustrated bruin finally disappeared into the woods.

It was really dusky now and I moved to the door to see more clearly. I felt the pressure of a soft sea breeze on my face and inhaled the enticing smell coming from the smoke house. With a happy sigh, I knew I could give Stu the answer he wanted to hear. Just as I turned to go inside, I was startled by the wild, inconsolable scream of a loon, a cry that is chilling when heard for the first time but which never fails to hold me spellbound.

"I'm hooked," I said, smiling at my husband as we stood together at the door. "I think we do need a change and a new car, but I'm coming back."

"I'm glad." His face lighted up with the brief comment. "Now let's light a lamp and make plans."

"Let's drive down the Alcan Highway," I said, all excited now with the anticipation of new roads to travel, new country to enjoy.

Two weeks later, in the middle of a black moonless night, we boarded the mailboat, Yakobi, with two cases of canned salmon and our clothes packed in duffle bags. Our boat and fishing gear were stored in one of the cannery buildings. Only a handful of people were left now in Tyee to see the mailboat off.

To me it was incredible how the skipper, Walt Sperl, could

navigate as he did on the blackest of nights and in all sorts of weather, often among reefs and islands. I stood on the stern deck for a while trying to see through the darkness but soon gave up, content to trust in the reputable seamanship of our friend from Juneau days.

The bunks were all located below and in the forward part of the vessel, so I lay down in one, fully dressed. One by one Stu and the other three passengers, all bound for Juneau, sought sleep also. I slept so soundly I was barely aware of several brief stops, no doubt at prospectors' or trappers' camps.

"We'll be here an hour," Walt said in the morning as he pulled into the dock at Kake, a native village of perhaps 500 people, on Kupreanof Island. A seemingly equal number of children and dogs played in the dirt streets, where obviously no litter laws were in effect. There was time to get off the boat and stretch our legs so we started off through the fog to see the town.

We walked by a number of large, well-built homes as well as the usual small nondescript dwellings, all weathered gray by the storms and salt-water air. The cannery buildings were closed but the large two-storey general store, owned by a white couple, was well-stocked and busy. After buying a few oranges and apples we stopped for a minute at the little post office and farther on was surprised to see a very creditable school building before circling back to the dock.

As the Yakobi wound its way out of the harbor, dotted with rocky reefs and small islands, Walt pointed out where there were other reefs now hidden by the incoming tide.

"Why would anyone build a town in such a rocky location?" I wondered aloud.

"Maybe a 100 years ago, a tribe of Indians decided that the dangerous reefs in the harbor and the waters adjacent to it would be an effective barrier against unfriendly tribes," one of the passengers suggested.

The trip was uneventful, although later in the day we passed huge chunks of floating ice and took some pictures. By late afternoon we docked in Juneau. Although I noticed many new faces on the streets, I felt right at home in the familiar surroundings and among old friends. My sister and family had moved south to Washington, so we didn't linger long in the city, anxious to get over the mountains before the snow came. We packed our car which had been stored in a friend's garage, and boarded a barge-type vessel for Haines at the north end of Lynn Canal. Several hours later we were following a gravel road over the Haines Cut-Off, the road that connects Alaska with the Alcan Highway in the Yukon Territory. On Chilkat Pass we stopped to watch a huge grizzly bear on the mountain side and to look at some short-stemmed white flowers, new to us, of unique beauty.

"It's too bad they'll bloom for such a short time," I said indicating the new snow that already covered the higher mountains like a topping of white frosting.

At Haines Junction we turned south, then passed through famous Whitehorse, capital of the Yukon Territory, the last city for several hundred miles. The mosquito season had passed with the coming of frosts, and recent rains had settled the dust on the miles and miles of washboard roads.

"Looks like we'll have twenty-five or thirty mile-an-hour roads all the way," Stu spoke a bit impatiently at the end of the first day.

"Yes, but we'll have lots of time to enjoy the gorgeous autumn colors," I said encouragingly. "Just look, as far as you can see in any direction, the aspens and birch trees are turning shades of yellow and orange."

Only recently had the road been opened for civilian traffic and although the gas stops were adequate, accommodations were meager as yet. There were a few lodge-type facilities in or near small settlements, but out in the boondocks, Quanset huts left behind by the U.S. Army were used for travelers, with only curtain partitions and either out-houses or chemical toilets. Some days we would see only three or four cars on the road.

"There's something on the road ahead," I said as we rounded a curve one afternoon.

"It's a bull moose and look at that rack of antlers," Stu said, slowing down. "It might be hostile, too." We approached slowly, unsure if the old male might challenge us.

"They get pretty mean sometimes during the mating season," he explained. The big animal stood facing us with its head lowered until we were about ready to back off, then it tossed the huge spread of antlers a couple of times and ambled off the road into the brush.

When a big fat grouse flew directly into the front of the car, Stu stopped and dressed out the lifeless bird and later we roasted it over a campfire beside a pretty little lake. That evening we saw mountain sheep close enough for a snapshot and in the morning ice coated the windshield.

We both breathed a sigh of relief when after being pulled through hub-deep mud by a bulldozer, we finally drove onto a surfaced highway near Edmonton.

"Now what do you think of the Alcan Highway," Stu asked at dinner that evening.

"It was great," I replied, "I wouldn't have missed it for anything. The wilderness is so big and peaceful, the coloring so fantastic, I'll never forget it."

"I liked it too," Stu agreed, "but I wouldn't want to do it over soon." Then he added, "and to think we didn't even have a flat tire."

Enjoying the luxury of a new Ford pick-up, we visited relatives and camped on the desert in sun-drenched Arizona for two months. When we visited the waterfront in San Francisco, the fishy smells and the familiar complaining cries of the sea gulls gave me a twinge of homesickness for Alaska. A glimpse of a snow-capped mountain reminded me of the towering peaks in the northland.

Often when traveling after dark I would stare longingly into the lighted windows of homes along our way and wonder what it would be like to have a real home like that, a permanent home that belonged to me and I to it. But would I trade our life in Alaska for it? Our simple manner of living, the vast wilderness with so much yet to be seen, the noble eagles, the wild animals and the quest for the big kings, would I give it all up to settle down in one place? Alaska always won.

The excitement of shopping in the big stores, mingling with crowds of people and driving with fast traffic, soon lost its appeal although we never tired of the fresh fruits and vegetables.

"It's about time for the hooters (grouse) to show up in Murder Cove," Stu unexpectedly remarked one morning. "How about it, are you ready to head north?"

"Oh yes," I answered, as eager to return to the northland I loved as I had been to leave months before. "It really has been a nice trip but I've had enough of the hubbub now. I like our slower pace in Alaska."

Weeks later we again traveled the fjord-like inland passage aboard the steamship, Northland, with the new, green pick-up on the forward deck. This time we disembarked at Petersburg, over a hundred miles south of Juneau and closer to Tyee. Although still eighty miles distant by boat, it would be more convenient for ordering supplies. We stored the pick-up in a private garage and after leaving freight to be sent on the mailboat we took a small plane to Tyee.

As the plane circled and glided down to the water I saw the patch of muskeg where we hunted and the stream with beautiful trout that few ever fished or knew of. Then just below was the spot on the beach where we saw a brownie with twin cubs and nearby were the big patches of wild asparagus. Smoke drifted from the chimney of the watchman's house and the tide still lapped gently on the beach in front of our cabin. This was home!

The freighter *Tongass* as it rests at dock on the Alaskan coast.

My sister Fern and I aboard the *Tongass* as it cruises along the Canadian coast on its way to Alaska. (April, 1939)

Fern and I stop for a break on the Mendenhall Glacier. (June, 1939)

A typical street in a Juneau residential area during the winter months.

Alaska can be both cold and beautiful at the same time. Here I go for a skate on frozen Auke Lake in the shadow of snow-capped peaks.

The Anchorage airport covered in snow with a mountain backdrop. (1940)

The local fire truck roars through the streets of Fairbanks in the middle of winter.

The cabin my husband and I always wanted.

A hunter who had a successful trip to Pelican, Alaska.

Dressed warm for the weather, I attempt to make friends with a husky.

When summer finally comes, we are able to grow a variety of produce for the Juneau Market.

Sweet peas and green peas thrive in the Alaskan soil.

Even Alaska does not have snow all year. This head of lettuce is part of our plentiful crop.

The fishery fleet brings its catch to cannery cabins such as those which line the shore in the background.

We like to eat salmon when it is smoked. Stu prepares a load of salmon for our smokehouse.

The mountains on Baranof Island sparkle under the sunlight of one of Alaska's bright summer days.

My husband Stu proved he was more than just an amateur fisherman with this seventy-three pound catch.

These five fifty pound king salmon represent one day's catch.

Much of Alaska remains untouched by man. Alaskan deer are readily able to roam Tyee Beach.

I almost matched Stu with a seventy-two pound king salmon of my own.

Some days we are really lucky. Two of these fish weigh over sixty pounds.

Some fish stories are bigger than others. This halibut weighs over 200 pounds.

I caught this fifty-five pound king salmon without any help.

This scenic stretch of road is part of the Alcan Highway.

We owned a precarious waterfront home in Tyee.

A female brown bear roams the shoreline with her two cubs close at hand.

Take your choice — blueberries and salmon berries grow abundantly in many parts of Alaska.

Warm Springs Bay, Alaska is a remote community with unmatched natural beauty.

Two large icebergs float aimlessly after breaking away from the glacier.

A trio of sea otters cleans the dock of any salmon scraps.

A fish-buyer's scow (red boat in the background) attracts a crowd of expectant fishermen in Tebenkof Bay.

These two men obviously enjoy their good crab haul.

The biggest of these salmon *only* weighed forty-five pounds.

Humming birds have an easier life with the help of man's work.

The sun sets gently over Tebenkof Bay, Alaska.

All photographs from the collection of Virginia Lechelt Neely.

18

Herding Whales

A year later, quite unexpectedly, we did buy our first home, small and lacking modern conveniences, but it was ours. When Pappy Short, a fisherman, offered us the two room cottage he had built, for $300 cash, we jumped at the chance. It was sturdily built with an enclosed porch and a large open deck and was set on pilings within the high-tide line, facing the inlet to Murder Cove. A twenty-foot tide brought the water under the front part of the house. Ours was the first building when approaching Tyee and the only privately-owned house. Since it was built on tidelands, no one could own the land.

Stu immediately plugged a hose into the cannery waterline so we at least had cold running water as well as electricity while the cannery was in operation. After the cannery closed for the winter we packed water from a creek or from an open well which was less desirable because it was brownish looking run-off water from the muskegs. This was much better than any of the cabins we had lived in so far but the outdoor privy in the woods at the back of the house was still a necessary part of the uncluttered life in the boondocks. I suggested remedying this situation be Stu's first assignment. Red checked curtains which I had sewed out of material from the mail order house and a red checked tablecloth to match added a cheerful touch to our new home.

I no longer worked in the cannery. Although the hours had been few, I was not free to go with Stu at all times to hunt, fish, pick berries or even gather wood for the smoke house. And I always felt a twinge of uneasiness when he left by himself; so many mishaps could happen in the woods or out on that big ocean. Not that I might prevent an accident but there was a better chance for anyone when not alone.

145

"You go today, I'd like to stay home," I told him once in a while when I longed for a few hours of my own to write letters, read or just be alone. But I soon realized I didn't relax much; I kept listening for the sound of an outboard motor or a step on the porch. It was better to go along than to stay home and worry.

I remember one night when he wanted to get a drift log that he had spotted earlier on the beach across the channel.

"Shall I go with you?" I asked.

"No, you go to bed. The tide won't be high enough to get it until about midnight. It'll only take me a half hour to tow it across to our float."

"Better take the flashlight," I advised.

"Alright, alright, now go to bed and quit worrying," he told me.

I was tired and was soon asleep. When I awoke I thought I had only nappd a few minutes but when I looked at the luminous dial clock, I was surprised to see it was an hour past midnight. I wondered if he had misread the tide table but I could hear the water sloshing under the house so knew the tide was at its peak.

"It's just taking longer than he thought," I reasoned. I went back to bed but couldn't sleep. Every few minutes I went out on the porch to listen for the sound of the motor or oars. It was too dark for me to see far but I knew Stu could manage in the partial light of a receding moon. I watched in vain for a flicker of his flashlight. At the time, we and the watchman's family were the only ones at Tyee.

By the time another hour had passed I was really worried. I walked to the edge of the porch time after time; I listened and my eyes strained to scan the shore. I prayed, then stared into the darkness again; I listened and prayed some more and looked again. I was getting frantic and had just started to dress when I heard him walking down the path to the house. He was whistling! Relieved but disgusted, I quickly crawled into bed and pretended to be asleep when he quietly undressed and slipped in beside me.

"I hope I didn't wake you when I came in," he said in the morning. "It was easier to tow with the tide than to buck it so I tied the log and boat to the cannery float. Then it was so nice I sat out there a while and watched some otters playing on the beach."

I stifled a yawn.

"You still tired after nine hours sleep?" he asked in surprise.

Weeks later we were gathering up our fishing gear one morning and about to leave the front porch when we heard whales blowing. We saw one after another moving up the channel, their dark backs surfacing in succession and their blowholes spouting steam at intervals. We counted twelve of the huge Humpbacks, the species most prevalent in southeast Alaska. Some were thirty to forty-feet in length and a few, half that size, we assumed to be young ones. They were evidently following a large school of herring that had moved into the channel.

"Let's chase those damn whales out of here — they'll ruin our fishing," Stu yelled as he grabbed his coat and hat and ran out the door.

I had no idea how he meant to stop one whale, let alone twelve. With some misgivings I followed him down the float to where our boat was tied. We cast off and he started the outboard motor and went full speed to the middle of the channel, ahead of the herd. As we zigzagged the boat back and forth in front of them, one after another turned and headed towards open water. We continued herding the docile creatures out a mile or more, then turned back, but had only gone a short distance when we realized that the whales had also turned and were starting back up the channel. Again we chased them out and I think by this time the whales were enjoying the game as much as Stu.

Finally they scattered or disappeared under water and we went back to start fishing only to find the whales had done their damage. They had caused the herring to leave the inlet and of course the salmon followed the herring. Whales do not interfere with salmon-fishing except to disturb the herring.

The king fishing had been good recently and especially so in the inlet when a large school of herring moved into Murder Cove. We were happy to see them come in. Now we could fish nearer home and in sheltered waters, safer for a sixteen-foot motor boat like ours, rather than several miles out on the open waters of Chatham Straits. But we should have known it couldn't last since seal, sea lions, porpoises and whales, as well as the salmon, follow and feed on the seemingly endless supply of herring.

For several days we saw few signs of herring and the salmon fishing was poor. The whales seemed to have left the area too. Then on a beautiful day, as only southeastern Alaska can be beautiful on a rare sunny day, we were lazily cruising down the inlet toward our favorite fishing grounds a couple of miles off shore. Across Chatham Straits the craggy snow-crested mountains on Baranof Island loomed conspicuously against the horizon. A brown bear was digging beach grass on the far side of the channel and farther on a doe and two fawns looked up from their browsing to gaze at us curiously.

We soon began to notice signs indicating herring in the vicinity, which meant salmon also. More than the usual number of bald eagles were perched in trees along the shore and some were circling out over the water then swooping down in an attempt to grasp a herring with their talons. Cormorants clung to rocks close to the water's edge waiting to dive after anything edible; farther out we saw the bobbing heads of a couple of seals or sea lions, always in search of food.

Stu shut the motor off and let the boat drift while we watched a flock of small birds, a species of sandpipers I believe. Like a moving cloud, they swooped and dipped and turned in unison; for just seconds at a time their wings caught the radiance of the sun and a glistening undulating wave seemed to move rapidly across the flock. Then with a graceful sweep downward the flock settled on the water and there was a steady chorus of low chirps while they fed on insects on the surface of the water. The little heads bobbed up and down with the rapid pecking motion of the long beaks reminding me of busy woodpeckers.

In the distance were large flocks of seagulls, some on the water, others complaining noisily, circling and diving to the surface of the water. Approaching nearer to where the squabbling gulls were fishing we saw what appeared like tiny ripples over a large area, and knew it was a huge school of herring swirling and flipping. As we slowly drew closer, we saw the water was black with herring. Sometimes these schools cover several acres to a depth of as much as a hundred feet.

Stu shut the big motor off and let the skiff drift into the mass of herring. (We always carried a small motor for a spare and also used it for trolling.) The flipping of millions of the small fish as they fed on algae, shrimp spawn or other minute forms of sea life sounded like the low roar of rapids heard from a distance. Since we needed fresh bait he moved to the bow of the boat to try to dip some with a landing net. We had shut off the little three-horse motor too, so the noise and prop turbulence in the water wouldn't frighten them away from the boat. I sat in the stern ready to operate the boat if we needed to move about.

Always when out on the water we kept watch for whales and whenever the motors were shut off we listened for the mildly explosive sound made by the forced discharge of their breath through the blow-hole, or we watched for what looked like spouts of steam as they exhaled. Sometimes we could see and hear them at least five or six miles away, judging by landmarks. When one slapped the water with its enormous tail it sounded like dynamite blasting. At times, we had seen one or more hurl its mighty body completely out of the water, falling back on its side creating an immense splash.

148

These antics might take place during courting; or to shake off barnacles clinging to their hides; or to stun a mass of herring; or just for fun. We never saw any evidence that the whales were hostile or aggressive but if a forty-ton whale was startled by coming up under a small boat or very close, it might dive head first and, as they often do when diving, slap its big tail which could be as wide as the length of our boat. The possibility of being crushed and the boat splintered was always present in our minds when these huge mammals were close by.

On this day we were so preoccupied with getting fresh bait we forgot about whales. The boat was drifting quietly when suddenly there was a big explosion only a few feet away as a huge whale leaped out of the water with its cavernous mouth wide open! It must have scooped up at least a half-ton of herring and some were dribbling from its mouth. (Whales do not always stun the herring, they sometimes just quietly slip under a big mass and come up with their mouths open.)

I sat there paralyzed! Stu shouted, "Start the motor! Start the motor!" I gave the cord a pull, the motor made one putt and stopped. It was out of gas. By this time the whale had swallowed its mouthful and as it sank to water-level again and started to move away it passed so close to the boat I could have laid my hand on that big black back with barnacles clinging to it. The big snout was covered with knobs and the eye next to the boat seemed to look right at me. Even in my fright I was amazed at how small that eye was in proportion to the size of the creature. I sat at the dead motor breathless, wondering if within a few seconds it would upend or crush us with a slap of that powerful tail. Stu quickly started the big motor with "Let's get the hell out of here!" Usually two or more whales travel together, and we didn't wait to see the second one. Still shaking as we left the whales behind, I vowed it was one adventure I didn't want again.

Later that same summer the friend we had gone to Angoon with several years before had guests out on his thirty-five foot troller. When they sighted a pod of whales nearby, he stopped the motor and let the boat drift so his friends could take pictures. Suddenly the troller was raised a short distance by an awful bump. It lurched over to one side a moment then settled back in its normal position just as a whale surfaced a few feet away. It was assumed to be an accident since the boat was not making any disturbance in the water. Although the boat was not badly damaged it was necessary to have it towed in by a passing vessel.

149

19

"Bearly Safe"

"Why can't we go deer-hunting today?" I asked Stu one morning in late summer. "We haven't had any fresh meat for weeks."

"I haven't seen any deer recently," he replied.

As we lingered at the table over our breakfast coffee we watched three bears on the beach across the inlet from our cabin. We had seen the same ones before and one time when we were on our way out to the fishing grounds Stu had guided the boat close to shore where the animals were digging in the grass. They watched us warily for a while, keeping close to the woods just above the high-tide line and as we approached nearer they lumbered over logs and into the brush. They always seemed quite clumsy but actually they could run as fast as a horse for a short distance. Sometimes one or the other stood up on his hind legs for a moment before disappearing into the woods.

All three were large adult bears. Two were quite dark but the third, a male, was somewhat larger than the other two and of an unusual light tan color with a darker mane around its neck that reminded me of a lion.

"I'm getting tired of fish," I continued to complain, "I'd like a big venison steak for dinner."

True, we had a variety of the best seafood in the world. Salmon, halibut, cod, snapper, crab and shrimp fresh out of the cold northern waters couldn't be beat. There was always some of Stu's delicious kippered salmon in the smoke-house to snack on. Nevertheless, after eating fish twice a day for weeks at a time — I drew the line at eating fish for breakfast — I thought it was about time to look for red meat.

Stu was gazing out the window, paying no attention to my complaints, when suddenly he tensed and gasped, "Look!" I looked across the channel and there was now another huge animal with the three bears. At first I didn't think it was a bear because it was so much larger than the others. Through my mind flashed thoughts of a moose, elk or horse, for just an instant, but at the same time I realized there were none of these on Admiralty Island. Moose inhabit the mainland and their long legs enable them to feed on water plants in bogs as well as strip the leaves from brush and trees to a height of seven or eight feet. Elk are not native to Alaska; some have been introduced onto other islands and horses are just not needed in this undeveloped wilderness.

"Just look at that monster!" Stu exclaimed. "The biggest bear I've ever seen!"

It must have been three times larger than the others. It looked as if their backs would only reach to the belly of the big one. While we were still staring in disbelief it went back into the woods.

"It's a wise old bruin, too," Stu said. "It doesn't linger long in the open."

Within the next few days two other people sighted what must have been the same brownie. One was an old timer, known for his fearlessness and reputation as a bear hunter. He was crossing a grassy meadow-like area along a creek. Topping a small rise he saw a bear so much larger than anything he had ever seen before that he immediately dropped flat to the ground. Although he carried his high-powered rifle as usual, he beat a hasty retreat, crawling on his hands and knees to keep out of sight in the tall grass. He vowed h e wanted nothing to do with that brownie.

For several days I continued to remind my husband what a tasty change of diet fresh venison would be, although I knew we should take advantage of every day the weather permitted us to fish.

One morning he put the coffee to brewing and as usual stepped out on the porch to assess the weather condition. It didn't hurt my feelings when he came back in and announced, "No fishing today. There's a north wind blowing down Chatham Straits and I can see white water. We'll go look for some of that red meat you've been hollering about, although the deer don't seem to be down on the beaches now."

I tumbled out of bed, cooked a mess of rolled oats, made toast and sugared a bowl of salmonberries, and soon we were on our way in the skiff with our rifles. It was a clear sunny day; the north wind wasn't all bad. (In the summer a north wind usually brought clear days.)

151

After leaving Tyee we stayed in sheltered waters by following the shore eastward. Our destination was a tiny, almost land-locked cove behind the Carroll Islands. These islands were little more than three huge rocks, with only a narrow kelp-covered passage between them through which only a small boat could navigate. I've always enjoyed the peacefulness and quiet of this pretty little hideaway. A vivid picture of the sky and evergreens mirrored in the clear water lent an added charm to this sunny day.

But it was meat we were after on this trip, not sight-seeing, so we approached the beach slowly and quietly stepping out of the boat. We pulled it up on the sandy shore far enough to keep it from drifting away. With our rifles ready we cautiously made our way up the grass covered bank, hoping to see a deer along the edge of a patch of open muskeg. We had replenished our meat supply here before.

Stu was ahead of me and when he topped the bank I noticed he raised his rifle at once. I could almost taste the venison chops already. But he stood still and motioned me to come quickly and quietly. As I moved up alongside him I saw not a deer, but a mother bear with two small cubs out in the middle of the muskeg. She had already smelled or heard us, and was heading towards the woods urging her young ahead of her with a smart smack of her big paw on their little rumps if either slowed down or looked behind. With anguished squeals they doubled speed and almost tumbled over their own feet as they disappeared into the brush.

Feeling more than a little uneasy I glanced around. I don't know where it came from but there was a big brownie loping along the edge of the water at the end of the cove, coming in our general direction.

"Let's get the hell out of here!" Stu blurted out.

"I'm going!" I shouted, already halfway to the boat. As he pushed us out away from shore we heard a crashing in the thicket only twenty feet from where we had been standing on the bank. Abruptly another brownie, the biggest of them all, lunged out of the brush!

"Wow! Look at the size of that animal!" Stu gasped. "I think it's the same one we saw across the inlet the other morning."

"It sure looks like it," I said as I stood fascinated and trembling. "Let's get out of here. I never dreamed a bear could be so big."

Astounded, we watched while the enormous brute angrily stomped around in a circle. Evidently it had heard and smelled us but didn't know just where the man-threat was located. We didn't wait for it to find out. Stu started the outboard and we putted toward home. I didn't say a word as I served fish for dinner.

A few days later our appetite for fresh meat again prompted us to try for a deer, but this time on a little island about three miles from Tyee by boat. Early in the morning we cruised into a tiny harbor at the entrance to a small heavily-wooded island, leaving a passageway so narrow that only small boats could pass through. Perhaps a quarter-mile across and not much more than a mile around, Stu felt this island was a safe place to hunt for deer since it was so small there wasn't enough feed on it of any kind for bear — or so we thought. So I felt no fear as we walked along the rocky beach in opposite directions, to meet at the other end, hoping by then one of us had made a kill.

Stu always carried his .30-06 but I liked my smaller .32 Winchester rifle. Since deer were not too plentiful close to the cannery, we sometimes found it necessary to make the trip around the island on more than one day before seeing one.

This morning we decided to watch a while from an abandoned cabin on the main island, only a short distance away, hoping deer might come out of the woods of the little island to feed on the beach grass, which they often did. We had just about decided to start walking the beach as before when Stu began, "Let's watch five more min—" He stopped in mid-sentence.

"Look!" he exclaimed. I followed the direction of his gaze. Out in the little harbor there was something moving in the water between the cabin where we hid and the island. It was soon close enough to make out a massive shaggy head and in another minute an enormous brown bear crawled up onto the beach of the little island and disappeared into the woods. We could only sit there staring at each other.

"Well I'll be damned!" Stu finally muttered. "I should have known better."

Bears do take readily to water and swim well. Only twice had I seen one swimming, both times it was between large areas of land.

Several days later Stu went over to the island where he had butchered a deer a month earlier.

"There isn't a thing left of that carcass except the hide," he told me when he returned. "Even the bones have been chewed up, only splinters left, and the earth is all torn up."

He looked at me, his face serious, unable to hide the shock and fear he felt.

"That bear was a big son-of-a-gun and you were out there with a little .32!"

153

I never went hunting on the island again and as far as we know, we never saw the same bear again.

20

Man Versus Herring

Season followed season with much the same activity. At times I thought there was never a dull moment, but there were days of dogged perseverence and hard work when I was glad to tear off the current sheet from the calendar, thus bringing closer the end of a fishing season.

Three years after we arrived in Tyee a fleet of herring seiners moved into the area, twelve to fourteen large boats each capable of holding eighty to a hundred tons. They would maneuver around slowly until they were positioned over a dense concentration of herring, then quickly string out the huge net in a circle. Gradually the net would be pulled in, decreasing the size of the circle and trapping the herring which were then poured into the hold of the ship by the ton. When loaded each went to Washington Bay, about twenty miles south, where the herring were processed into fertilizer. Probably 2000 tons were taken during a season.

The local residents and fishermen signed petitions and sent them to Washington D.C. trying to stop, or at least limit, the seining in Chatham Straits. The only result was a directive from the Fish and Wildlife office in Washington stating that salmon did not feed on herring. What? All the fishermen used herring for bait and many a time, as we landed a big salmon on the floorboards of the boat, herring spewed from its mouth. More than once when we were short of bait, Stu had cut open the stomach of a salmon just caught and retrieved a herring or two still undamaged by the fast-acting digestive juices typical of any fish. Yet the authorities in Washington D.C. were informing the public that salmon do not eat herring, hence the seiners supplying the fertilizer factory posed no hazard to the salmon industry.

Year by year the herring schools became smaller and consequently the salmon runs declined steadily. Finally the seiners cleaned up the herring for miles around and the processing plant closed. We seldom had any problem jigging herring for fresh bait but now we were becoming apprehensive.

"I think I'll build a little bait box," Stu said one evening, "then if I get a chance to dip some with the net, I can transfer them into the box and we'll have live bait on hand all the time."

He made a three-foot box of wire mesh and anchored it two or three feet under water near the float in front of our cabin. When we saw herring flipping at the edge of a kelp patch, he let the skiff drift quietly into the small school until he could scoop up some with a dip net, then dumped them into a tub of water and hurried to transfer them into the bait box. Just two days later as we started out fishing he decided to pull up the bait box and take along a few to use until he had time to jig some. We were dumbfounded to see a bunch of skeletons in the box. Sea lice had picked them clean. Obviously the herring couldn't be confined in such a small area.

The tiny water animals commonly known as sea lice are a species of amphipods. Belonging to the same group of crustaceans as shrimp, lobsters and crabs, they have hard shells, jointed bodies, and are a little larger than a grain of rice. Hordes of these vicious lice will attack any fish or other sea life hooked, trapped or with mobility otherwise limited.

Later we learned from halibut fishermen that they never left their skates of gear (long lines with hooks placed at intervals) down more than two hours because the damage done by sea lice to the hooked halibut could render them unmarketable. In twenty-four hours sea lice could completely devour a large halibut, leaving only the skeleton and skin.

Not long after the bait box incident we learned of the inevitable — the cannery would close down permanently after the season of 1954 was over. There would be no cold storage and most discouraging for us, no place to sell our salmon. Already the majority of the trollers had left to seek better fishing in other areas. There wasn't much chance we could provide enough salmon to justify a fish buyer coming in to Tyee regularly. Buyers needed to be where there were many trollers fishing.

"Let's take a walk up the hill," I suggested after we both sat with long faces drinking coffee the day we learned of the closure. We quietly followed a trail, Stu ahead as usual with his gun. Breaking out of the trees, we started across a large patch of spongy muskeg dotted with a few scrubby spruce trees, dwarfed and twisted by the ruthless elements.

"I've never noticed before that the muskeg is so colorful," I commented. "It looks like it's covered with flowers." Already the leaves of small plants common to the muskeg were turning a variety of soft autumn hues and on a sunny day gave the illusion of being flowers.

We carefully avoided the many water holes typical of muskegs, some as much as two feet across. Idly, I found a dead branch about six feet long and failed to touch bottom with it in several of the holes. Minutes later I quietly walked up to a spotted fawn curled up asleep on the sod. I watched it for a moment and even patted it before it awoke startled and half-dazed from sleep. It stood trembling for just an instant before it bounded away into the forest. Later I was told that a fawn has no odor of its own so as to protect it from predators. I've always wondered if I unwittingly stamped the little creature with the man-smell, causing it to come to a tragic end.

When we came to an open ridge we sat to rest awhile. Far below we saw the cannery buildings and beyond, the kelp patches, the reef and the area of comparatively shallow water between shore and the main stream of Chatham Straits which we called the 'flats'.

"We were lucky," Stu said. "We came to Tyee in time to have several years of fabulous fishing."

"Do you think it's over?" I asked.

"Not altogether, there'll be a few herring and where there's herring there'll be salmon. But we've had an ideal set-up here; the cannery, the cold storage to sell to, the store, and a nice place to live. I'm afraid we'll never see it just like this again."

And just when we've bought our own home," I said, indignant at the thought of again having to pull up stakes and start over. I gazed over at the rugged mountains crested with snow. I thought of the words, 'I will lift up mine eyes unto the hills . . .'; words that flashed into my mind so often since this great wilderness had become my home. From where we stood I could see the blue ice of small glaciers in some of the canyons. What looked like a huge snow slide extended down to the high tide line, spilling from a steep canyon like sugar from a broken sack.

"This is one of the prettiest places in which we've lived," I went on, turning to Stu.

"I'm not going to give up yet. What do you say we stay a couple of years and see what happens?" Stu said fervently, putting his arm around my shoulders.

"I'm not anxious to move again and clean up more dirty cabins," I replied quickly. "I like it here, but can we make it pay?" "I'll be satisfied to make expenses, and it'll be a good life," he answered.

"We'll get by," I agreed. "We've done well here and have a little surplus in the bank. But I feel sorry for some of the other fishermen with big boats and a big investment; it'll be tough with the cannery closed."

"Yes," Stu responded, thoughtfully. "Looks like the salmon industry has nothing but trouble ahead. And to think greed is at the bottom of it all. The traps get the young salmon that should grow up to spawn; the creek robbers take those going up to spawn, the seiners scoop up the herring and the big interests down in the states that own the canneries and traps aren't concerned with the future of the salmon runs. They just want to make money right now."

We spoke of the fact that Alaska was still a territory and governed by the people in Washington D.C. who had little knowledge of true conditions in the far north and were influenced by the lobbyists of the big fish companies. Alaskans had no vote. When, a few years later, in 1959, Alaska did become a state, the traps were immediately outlawed but much of the damage already done was irreversible.

While we sat there, a freighter came into sight and steamed up the channel to Tyee, the huge vessel looking out of place in the narrow but deep-water harbor. We watched a small boat assisting in maneuvering the freighter by pushing against one side of the ship. It always looked like some kind of joke to me, to see the tiny outboard boat, nose against the vast bulk of the large vessel, its propeller churning up the water as it strained to slowly but surely swing one end of the huge freighter in close to the dock.

"Shall we go down and watch the excitement?" Stu asked.

"Sure, maybe there will be a late newspaper or some fresh fruit aboard," I replied, starting down the trail.

21

King Salmon and No-See-Ums

On a sunny day in late June during the summer of 1955 we were looking forward to a visit by my Uncle Dan Birkemeier and his wife, Evelyn, from Milwaukie, Oregon. The cannery no longer operated, so the total population of Tyee at this time was five — the cannery watchman and his wife and child plus my husband and I. Our footsteps echoed through the empty buildings and the lush growth of rain-drenched grass and brush was already threatening to take over.

"That doesn't sound like the old Goose," Stu commented. We were standing outside the house scanning the sky, listening to the drone of a plane in the distance. The Grumman Goose, ten-seater passenger planes, dependable and with tremendous power, had proved well adapted for mountainous southeastern Alaska. They made regularly scheduled trips to the cities and some of the villages. There were also many non-scheduled trips to small camps, isolated homes, fishing villages or wherever there was a need for transportation. When the regular passenger planes were all busy, small shuttle planes, some of questionable vintage, were sometimes substituted to carry people to their destinations.

The watchman had offered us the use of one of the nearby cannery cabins for our guests. It contained a small cast-iron stove and a bed. We added bits of furnishings we found in other empty cabins: a cracked mirror, a couple of old chairs and a dresser fashioned from two orange crates and covered with a turkish towel. Dish towels made do for window curtains. The finishing touch was a large bouquet of wild columbine I picked early on the day of their arrival and arranged in an empty peanut butter jar.

We weren't surprised when a small plane instead of the

distinguished Goose, came into view, circled, glided down and taxied to the float. Uncle Dan had fared well, he sat up front with the pilot. My aunt, however, was in the back seat, wedged between a couple sacks of flour and a quarter-side of beef. The pilot helped her out somewhat shaken but cheerful. The plane had been so loaded it couldn't take off from the water until part of the freight was removed, including our guest's baggage which the pilot promised to bring the next day. The fresh meat took priority.

With everyone trying to talk at once we finally made it to the house and enjoyed a cup of coffee while catching up on the latest family news.

"I'll fix lunch while you folks get settled in your cabin and take a look around," I told them after the chattering began to run down.

"Just follow the trail to the left of the cabin," I answered Evelyn's inquiring look as she went out the door. "I told you it would be rough up here," I added, smiling.

"You didn't scare us," she said cheerfully. "We have been looking forward to this trip and excited to spend some time in your Alaskan wilderness, a hundred miles from a city. Imagine that!" It would be a unique experience for them. No phones, no roads, no cars, no hot running water, no plumbing, and no corner store. However there were some pluses: a quiet, unshackled, simple sort of life, snow-capped mountains towering over their own reflections in the blue waters of Chatham Straits, time to observe the various types of wildlife, pick wildflowers, stroll on the beach and listen to the lonesome cry of the loon in the evening.

"I hope you both like seafood because we have lots of it here," I said when we finally gathered around the table for a lunch of kippered salmon, cheese, pickled kelp, wild asparagus salad and home-made bread.

"We do," Dan answered. "And it must be great coming from the ocean to the table." Then he admitted with a grin, "I already sampled Stu's kipper when I went by the smokehouse."

"How about beer bits for supper?" Stu suggested. "I'll cut up the halibut we caught yesterday."

"What's beer bits?" Evelyn asked a bit dubiously.

"I make a batter," I explained, "like for baking powder biscuits only I make it thinner and use beer for the liquid. Then I dip little strips of halibut in the batter and deep fry or just fry them in oil in a skillet and turn each piece until brown all around."

"It's delicious," Stu added.

"Sounds interesting," Evelyn agreed. "I think I'm going to learn of some new dishes out here in the wilds."

Since it was a beautiful day and the waters calm, the men were anxious to try fishing. But Dan had nothing to wear except the good clothes he was wearing when he arrived. However he wasn't about to let that stop him and when Stu offered his rain coat and pants the problem was solved. Who cared if they were a bit short in the arms and legs because he was six foot two and Stu five foot ten? Away they went.

I washed the dishes in a dishpan of water that had been heating on the stove while Evelyn swept the floor. Then I kneaded down the bread dough that I had set earlier and formed it into individual loaves to rise again.

"How do you keep up with the housekeeping and go fishing too?" Evelyn asked.

"The house cleaning really doesn't amount to much in these small cabins," I replied. "This is the worst chore," I added while rinsing out some clothes that had been soaking in a washtub. "I do get exasperated with washing and drying clothes in the wintertime."

"Do you can salmon?" she inquired noticing the pressure cooker in the corner.

"Yes, we can salmon and venison too, sometimes two or three days at a time. Stu prepares the fish and I tend the cooker. We try to do it on stormy days when we can't fish."

"How have you taken care of your salmon this year with the cold storage closed down?"

"With the big herring schools gone, we're not catching near as many salmon this year. So far other fishermen that happened by have taken some to town for us and we sent some in on the mailboat which still comes once a week. Sometimes a fish buyer comes in but we can't depend on it so it's not a very satisfactory set-up here now. We can and smoke what we don't sell."

We pulled a few radishes and green onions from Stu's tiny garden and opened a can of green beans to go with the beer bits and fried rice I had planned for supper to be topped off with fresh fruit our guests had brought with them. We then enjoyed a long walk along the beach wondering how the fishermen were doing. I really didn't expect they would have much luck as the salmon had been scarce so far that season.

When we heard the boat coming late in the afternoon we met the men at the beach. As Stu maneuvered the boat in close I saw the big grin on Dan's face and a moment later when he stepped out he used all his strength to lift out a huge king salmon and drop it on the sandy beach. We were all thrilled admiring the big silver-sided fish, each one making a guess at the weight before I ran to the house for the scales and cameras. Dan was elated when it weighed an even sixty-four pounds, by far the largest salmon he had ever caught or seen.

"And to think," he remarked, "I just left Portland this morning. Tomorrow, I want to eat a steak from a sixty-four pound salmon."

"And you can help me kipper the rest to take home with you," Stu promised.

Talking over the day's events at the supper table Stu told how, as they were headed out to the kelp patches looking for signs of herring, they saw a flock of sea gulls noisily circling over a rip-tide. That's where they put their baits down and it wasn't long before they found action. We felt encouraged, hoping the big schools of herring were beginning to show up as usual.

"What in the world do you do way out here if someone gets hurt or sick?" Evelyn asked later watching me apply mercurochrome and bandaids to some scratches on Stu's fingers. "Do you keep any emergency supplies on hand?"

"Only the usual thing like bandaids, adhesive tape, antiseptic ointments, Vicks Rub and aspirin. Mostly we watch out for fish poisoning which is an infection often caused by scratches from the teeth when cleaning fish. We've never had a bad accident yet and if we did I suppose we'd try to flag down a passing boat or plane."

"How could you do that?" she asked. I explained that hoisting something white on a pole or from the top of a building was a sign of help-needed and bush pilots or boat skippers quickly responded to such a signal.

"That is if we're lucky and they see it. It's one of the risks we have to accept if we want to live in the boondocks," Stu added.

"And Stu always keeps a bottle of whisky on hand," I said, "since there are no snakes in Alaska, he says it's for mosquito bites."

"We need fresh water," I announced after supper. I used the brownish-looking water from the open well back under the trees for washing and dishwater but didn't like the muskeg drainage for cooking or drinking.

"Might as well go along for the ride," Stu suggested to Evelyn and I as he carried several empty cans and jugs to the boat. Moving slowly through the shallow water at the head of the cove, we went up the creek beyond the reach of tide water and filled the containers from the clear cold stream.

"What in the world made a path like that?" Dan asked in astonishment, pointing to a well-beaten path nearly two feet wide through four foot high grass, ending at the creek only a few feet from the boat.

"Bear," Stu answered, "and big ones too."

"Let's get out of here!" Evelyn urged.

A few days later the men went out as usual but my aunt and I decided to stay ashore and rest. Several days bouncing around in a small boat was tiring. Evelyn was mixing a batch of bread and I had just finished washing my hair in a basin on the washstand outside the door when I noticed a sudden disturbance in the water a short distance from the float in front of the house. A small mass of herring was flipping out of the water in sudden rushes and in the midst of them was a silver streak as large salmon broke water. I realized at once that a school of salmon were following the herring into the inlet.

"Evelyn! Come quick!" I called, but her hands were in the bread dough. I threw my towel aside, ran down the ramp and jumped into a heavy plank cannery skiff we had been using for an extra boat. While I quickly cut a spinner from the side of a herring and baited a hook, I heard the surge of water as the salmon continued to rush through the herring, stunning and crippling some by hitting them with their tails, then devouring the cripples. That's why cut spinners resembling crippled herring made such terrific bait.

Hurriedly I untied the skiff and rowed out a few feet then dropped my bait in the water and let out line. I had just picked up the oars again when all of a sudden the reel started buzzing and the line running out at miles per hour. I dropped the oars, jumped up, grabbed the pole and got a finger on the spool to prevent a backlash; it was unwinding so fast. Nearly always a hooked salmon will head for deep water, but luckily this one headed up the inlet toward more shallow water. Since we used only fifteen pound line and a twelve pound test leader it was impossible to stop one or even slow it down.

The tide was carrying me in the opposite direction from the way the fish was going and I knew if I didn't get the outboard motor started and follow it, I'd soon run out of line. I jerked the starting cord with one hand, holding the pole in the other. All the while the no-see-ums were attacking me viciously. They were all over my face and hands, under my glasses and in my mouth if I didn't keep it shut. I was more than busy as I steered the boat trying to follow the king as it circled one way and another, while swiping at the no-see-ums and at the same time reeling in line whenever I gained a little.

Instead of sounding as it would have in deeper water, the big

Tyee was wearing itself out in fast runs. Several times I had it so close I could see it five or ten feet under water, only to have it take off again. It looked like a monster! I feared I could never land it, guessing it to be nearly fifty pounds. Glancing toward shore to see if there was any sign of help coming, I saw Evelyn standing on the porch waving a dish towel!

Finally the runs became shorter. The king was tiring. So was I. I shut off the motor and slowly and carefully reeled it in closer and closer. The pole was almost bent double as I tried to keep the line taut with one hand and slip the long handled landing net under that great fighter with the other. On the third try I succeeded, dropped the pole and grabbed the rim of the net with both hands. I had no idea how I could lift it in without tipping the boat, but I thought, "I just can't lose it now." Bracing one foot against the top edge of the heavy flatbottomed skiff, I gave a big heave and slid my captive beauty over the side and into the boat.

"Whoopee!" Evelyn yelled. I slumped on the seat shaking all over. I was too tired to cheer.

Now that the tension was over I soon recovered and being a greedy fisherman I foolishly baited both poles thinking I might as well drag a couple of baits on the way into the float. A breeze had come up blowing the no-see-ums away. It had taken about an hour to land my prize and I supposed by this time the marauding salmon had scattered the herring and left the cove. The tide had carried me halfway down the inlet toward open water. I saw no more sign of herring so jumped a foot off the seat when one of the poles dipped suddenly and the reel unwound with a screech. Dropping the oars I grabbed the pole just as the other reel started singing. I stood there dumbfounded, helpless to do anything with what I felt were again big fish. So I sacrificed the one headed out to sea, propped that pole against the side of the boat with the butt end firmly wedged under a seat so it couldn't go overboard, and concentrated on the other which was circling, giving me a chance to alternately pump the pole up and down and reel in the slack.

I was getting tired and wondering if I could outlast this one when I heard the welcome sound of a motor boat. Stu and Dan were coming toward me. I could imagine their surprise to see me out in the middle of the channel playing a salmon when I was supposed to be relaxing ashore. Stu eased his boat alongside and stepped into mine almost falling over the big king lying in the middle of the boat. With more than a little satisfaction I watched as he stopped short in disbelief.

"Where in hell did that come from?" he blurted out, for a moment not even associating it with me. He would never have

164

believed I could land one that size all by myself. Neither would I.

"Come on, get moving, get on the motor!" I ordered, with a touch of well deserved arrogance, I thought. Our system of team-work, developed in years of fishing together proved quite efficient and soon we landed my second salmon. The one headed out to sea had never stopped, it took all the line. I'll always believe the one that got away was the biggest.

Evelyn was eagerly waiting on the float with the scales. My first catch weighed fifty-five pounds, ten ounces, the last forty-eight. The men's empty boat in no way dampened their enthusiasm over my good luck. I was a sight, my face and hands red and swollen from no-see-ums bites but I was happy.

"We need ice for those salmon," Stu said after an early supper of canned venison, fried potatoes, hot biscuits and more wild asparagus. This time we cooked it like greens.

"Where will you get ice?" Dan asked.

"We go across the straits to Warm Springs Bay on Baranof Island and get chunks from the frozen snow slide. Its just like ice," Stu explained.

Dan and Evelyn chose not to go along because of the everpresent possibility of a blow and rough water causing us to be stranded for hours or maybe all night on the other side of the straits. Dan would enjoy fishing for Dolly Varden trout from the float and Evelyn said she'd just rest and watch him from the porch.

"We'll bring enough ice for ice cream, too," I shouted as we shoved off.

The water was smooth and we made the fifteen-mile crossing in less than an hour. Just inside the Bay, Stu turned into a short break in the shoreline and eased up to a bank of frozen snow and ice at the bottom of a snow-filled ravine. I held the boat in place while he climbed out on the bank and chopped off several chunks. He slid them carefully into the boat and covering all with gunny sacks we were soon on our way home.

"It's been a big day and I think we're all tired and ready to hit the sack," Stu said after the salmon had been well-iced. "Sometime I'll tell you some fish stories about the big one that got away."

"Today we have a crab feed," Stu announced the next morning after we had finished our hotcakes and bacon with wild currant jelly.

Early in the afternoon, at low tide, with the boat drifting, the men speared eight large crabs and cooked them in a wash-boiler over a fire on the beach. I saw them both slapping at the deer flies and was glad we had picked enough greens for salad earlier. Three or four times the size of a house fly, a deer fly doesn't just sting, it takes a bite out of the flesh and can be felt through ordinary clothing. It is painful and sometimes causes an infection. We were relieved when it started to rain and they disappeared. The frequent rains can be a blessing during the short period when the pests are bothersome.

"That's the best crab I've ever eaten," both of our guests agreed when we had just about emptied the big kettle of cracked crab that had been placed in the middle of the table.

"Where's the ice-cream?" Stu demanded with mock gusto.

"You're going to help clean up this crab-mess first," I informed him, "then the Pierces are going to join us for ice-cream topped with salmon berries."

While the crabs were cooking I had made up the cream mixture, using canned milk, eggs and gelatine, and the men hand-turned the freezer which I borrowed from our only neighbors.

"Don't you ever get lonesome up here? It seems so far away." Evelyn asked the evening before the plane was to come and take them to Juneau where they would transfer to a larger plane to Seattle.

"I never think about being lonesome," I told her. "I don't know of any place else I'd rather be and there's so much to see and do here. I do enjoy visitors and people to talk with when boats sometimes stop overnight. But I don't really get lonesome. Oh, maybe just a teeny bit once in a while."

"Stu, I want to hear those fish stories you said you'd tell us before we go," Dan reminded him while he finished tying up a package of kippered salmon.

"Let Virginia tell it."

So I told them about two incidents, vivid in my mind to this day, that happened in years past.

Although I believe we caught more than our share of exceptionally large king salmon, there were times when the big one got away. As far as we are aware we know of no others who consistently landed as many of the really big ones as we did on sport-fishing gear. However this was little consolation when we lost a battle with a great fighter.

On one occasion we were fishing off Aaron Island in Lynn Canal in 1948 while living at Auke Bay near Juneau. In this area salmon were averaging about fifteen or twenty pounds; a forty pounder was unusual. We were still using some old wartime reels in 1947 and '48 which gave us a lot of trouble. They were not made of stainless steel, but of inferior and plastic materials that caused the spools to backlash and the line to get stuck in the gears. Good new reels were scarce on the market.

By the middle of the afternoon we had a fair catch in the fish box and were about to call it a day when all of a sudden Stu's pole bent into a half circle and his reel started unwinding with a loud screech.

"Get on the motor, I think it's a big one!" he yelled at me. I hurriedly reeled in my line and started the outboard motor.

"My line's half gone already," he said excitedly as the salmon took off with great speed toward deeper water. I headed the boat in the direction of his line.

"Step on it, I haven't much line left!" I opened the throttle still more and soon he was reeling in line as we gained on the king. It was important not to gain too fast, causing a slack in the line and increasing the chances of the hook coming loose.

The speed and strength with which this salmon was traveling indicated it was larger than anything we had hooked for some time — maybe ever. After twenty minutes or so I turned off the motor and let the boat drift. The king was straight down now, very deep, but Stu was pumping the pole up and down, reeling in as he gradually and very carefully eased it upward. By this time we were at least a mile from where we started.

After several more runs, shorter each time, we knew the salmon was tiring. Both of us were tensely watching to catch a glimpse of the big fighter as it neared the surface.

"Get the dip-net handy," Stu nervously instructed me, "put the poles and other stuff out of the way." I also moved the gun to a safe place. We always kept one on the boat to scare sea lions away and as a protection from bear if we went ashore. Sea lions had been known to follow a hooked salmon right up to a boat and even attempt to climb in.

"Look!" Stu gasped, "That's the biggest king I've ever seen!"

I turned and just had a glimpse of it when he said anxiously, "Here you take the pole, I'll net it." I'm sure he did the right thing as I could not have handled such a big one. I took the pole from him, being careful not to let the line go slack for even a moment.

Just as he cautiously but quickly reached out with the dip net, the monster made a sudden fast lunge, missed the net, the pole jerked down, the reel backlashed, the line snapped and that beautiful silvery streak was gone.

Stu pulled the net back slowly and looked at me. He couldn't understand why the line broke.

167

"Backlash," I said in a weak voice.

"Where's my gun?" he suddenly asked sharply. For a moment I wondered who he was going to shoot, me or himself. Then he added, "Oh, there it is," and I realized he was afraid that in the excitement it might have fallen into the water. He then deliberately threw the wartime reel, pole and all overboard.

"Should have done that long ago," he muttered. "Let's go home.

We guessed that salmon must have weighed between sixty and sixty-five pounds.

Several years later and a hundred miles away from that spot we hooked another big one after four seasons of fabulous fishing for the big Tyees off the southern tip of Admiralty Island in Chatham Straits. The salmon were much larger here, and about ninety percent of them were red as compared to seventy-five percent white in the Juneau area. Because of the higher price of reds, this was a much more profitable location for fishing.

Many times we came in with ten or fifteen king salmon, half of which weighed from fifty to sixty-five pounds. By this time my husband had a 75-pound, 12 ounce and a 73 pound, 10 ounce king to his credit and my largest were 72 and 70 pounds. There were also a lot of halibut in this area, some over 200 pounds. So one day when we were fishing in a deep gut right off Point Gardner, Stu hooked what he thought was a big halibut. It didn't make much of a run but stayed deep and heavy, typical of the bottom fish. However a couple of times it circled and came up part way which is not typical.

"Maybe it is a salmon," Stu said, perplexed. "If so it's a big one." Again it went to the bottom and hung there like a dead weight.

For nearly an hour he fought with it, raising it some distance several times, always carefully as we still didn't know what it was. His pole would bend almost double as he tried to work it up. I expected the pole to break any moment. Finally he handed it to me saying, "I'll try to bring it up by hand, you reel in the slack line." This was the way we usually handled a big halibut. He could put more pressure on the line by hand than with a limber pole. Since by now we were almost sure it was a halibut and both were so preoccupied, I hadn't thought of putting the dip net within easy reach. It is impossible to net a big halibut or get one in the boat. They are hard to kill and so powerful when flopping around they can do much damage to anything in the boat. Stu always shot a big one in the head when he got it up close then towed it behind the boat. At this time halibut were out of season

168

so when he saw it he would just break the leader line.

He was on his knees at the side of the boat leaning over the edge and watching intently as he gained line inch by inch.

"It's getting close," he said. "It's a king! a hell-uv-a big one!" Now we both got so excited we did everything wrong. I reached for the net while trying to hold the reel and pole with one hand and in so doing I let a little slack in the line which somehow looped around the end of the pole. Stu was trying to hold the line taut with one hand and reach for the net with the other. At the critical moment the big lunker made a run for it and the line snapped at the loop.

"It's gone," he said in a woebegone voice. Venting his disappointment and anger with a few choice cuss words, he threw his hat on the floor of the boat, stomped on it, then sat down and started getting things in order again. In less than five minutes he was whistling. I sat down hard and looked at him aghast! How could he whistle at a time like this, after just losing the biggest salmon he had ever hooked? I was wallowing in the depths of despair and self-pity with no intention of getting out of the doldrums for hours, maybe days.

22

Close Squall

The satisfaction we felt in owning our own home was short-lived. By the end of another season we reluctantly admitted we could no longer make expenses due to the decline in the salmon run and the unfavorable conditions we encountered in handling and selling our fish.

Knowing one of his stops was at a logging camp where any kind of housing was badly needed, we had told Walt Sperl, owner of the mailboat Yakobi, that the house would be for sale at the end of the fishing season. On his next trip to Tyee he handed us a check for $300, the same amount we had paid for it, from a logger with the understanding he would have it towed over to his camp, on a barge, when we left. Nothing was in writing, only a verbal agreement through our friend on the mailboat.

We moved to Petersburg the following winter, a city of perhaps 2000 people on Mitkof Island at the entrance of Wrangell Narrows and about eighty miles from Tyee. We rented a small house at Scow Bay where we fished a run of salmon early in the spring. Although we did well the weather was so nasty I didn't enjoy it much. Often we fished in the cold rain, sometimes mixed with snow, until my fingers were so cold I could hardly strike a match when I went inside to start a fire while Stu cleaned the salmon.

"At least there's no bugs to bother us," he said once when he came in with his face red and nose dripping.

"I don't want much of this," I grumbled.

We couldn't forget Tyee and two years later we decided to spend one more summer there for fun if nothing else. Partly, too, out of curiosity; we wondered if the herring had come back.

170

"Weather looks O.K. . . . all ready to shove off?" Stu asked untying the line from the dock in Petersburg as I settled into a little space left on the forward seat of our boat. Our sleeping bags and some clothing were packed in the bow under the deck where they would keep dry. There were water-tight cans of food and several five-gallon cans of gas for the motor. We were traveling light, having loaded the bulk of our summer supplies and fishing gear on Duke Short's boat. He was now making the mail run. With good luck we would beat him to Tyee and be there to take care of our freight when it arrived because there was no one living there now to help out.

The tide was in our favor as the boat bounced through the rip-tides of Wrangell Narrows into the smoother waters of Frederick Sound, the weather calm but cloudy. Although it was June we wore wool clothing because it was never warm traveling in an open boat on the icy waters of Alaska. We even passed several huge chunks of floating ice. The jagged edges of the tiny icebergs sparkled like clear crystal; the thicker and more dense parts were pale sea-green and the areas where they had recently broken from the glacier were a deep blue.

We followed the shoreline of Kupreanof Island, watching for signs of wild life. Deer browsed in the beach grass, a mink came out of the water in one place with something in its mouth possibly a shellfish of some kind, and clambered over the rocks toward the brush. Twice we saw a black bear. Often we spotted the white head of a bald eagle perched in a tree, ever watchful for a potential meal.

"Look!" I shouted when a school of playful porpoises raced alongside the skiff, breaking water just at the right moment to give us a cold shower.

"But I wish they'd play their jokes somewhere else," I muttered, wiping the water off my face and glasses. I've always felt these showers were not unintentional.

Once we slowed down to watch several humpback whales creating quite a disturbance. One leaped clear of the water then fell back into the sea with a resounding splash. Others dived head first while their enormous tails flailed the water with such force that it sounded like a series of explosions. We saw no herring around so wondered if the whales were just feeling frisky or had some more serious reason for their vigorous antics. A whale supposedly weighs approximately a ton to a foot of its length and I couldn't imagine them playing like kittens or puppies.

"Best we keep moving. You know how quickly these waters can rough up," Stu warned.

171

the safe and comfortable life of the landlubber. Dusk was falling and the storm worsening when we finally drew near to shore.

"Look!" Stu shouted, pointing ahead. With relief I saw what appeared to be a small sheltered cove. While I watched over the bow for rocks, he slowly and carefully eased the boat out of the turbulent waves, through the narrow entrance into calm water.

"Am I ever glad to get in here," I said, my heart still pounding.

Stu shook his head in disbelief. "It was flat when we started across. I had no idea it would stir up so damn fast."

We decided against going ashore because the beach was rocky and also there was danger from brown bears which we knew were numerous on the island. By the time we anchored, had a cup of coffee, some hardtack, a dry hard biscuit that keeps indefinitely, and a candy bar, it was raining steadily. Weary from our rough ride, we made ourselves as comfortable as possible propped against some of the luggage. Our slickers kept us dry and warm. Drowsy and relaxed I felt as though the darkness of the short summer night had spread its protective mantle over us. I even enjoyed the soft patter of the rain on the water, the peacefulness of this secluded refuge and the gentle rocking motion of the skiff.

Gradually the sounds of the night invaded the quietness: the hoot of an owl and a faint answer in the distance, the rustle of a small animal in the brush along the beach, and the loon's eerie cry. The loon or diver as it is so aptly known is a most interesting bird. It can dive deeper and stay underwater longer than any other bird. It lives almost continuously in water and feeds largely on fish which it can outswim and even chase to a depth of more than a hundred feet.

We slept fitfully, shifting our positions often. In June dawn comes early in the north and as I lay there looking towards the main channel I noticed a large dark form right in the middle of the entrance through which we had come. It seemed to disappear for a few moments, then reappear. I thought it was a whale but as the dawn turned to daylight we were both amazed to see a huge rock. The ocean swell covered it, then receded a little more each time as the tide ebbed.

"Well I'll be darned!" Stu exclaimed. "We must have barely cleared that last night. We're lucky it was high tide."

About 10:30 the storm lessened considerably and we started out slowly, following the shore of the island. The mailboat was due in Tyee in mid-afternoon and we were anxious to be there to take care of our supplies. When we had only about three miles to

172

Soon we passed Portage Bay, the last protected harbor until we rounded the end of the island. A little later we stopped and let the boat drift while Stu refilled the gas tank from one of the five-gallon cans. I poured us each a cup of coffee from a thermos and we sat for a few minutes looking at the shoreline before he started the motor again. The beach here was very rocky and dense forest grew down to the water-line. As we went on and neared Pinta Point, I noticed Stu looking to the north frequently. Following his gaze I saw a dark streak at the water-level in the far distance. Big waves and a rough sea from an approaching gale sometimes appears like a dark bank or wall across the water or it can be caused by rip-tides. Anyway, the sight of that ominous sign always caused me to scan the shoreline for a sheltered hole to duck into.

In answer to my anxious look he shouted above the motor noise, "It doesn't look bad yet, too far away."

He opened the throttle a little more and we were soon rounding Kupreanof Island and heading west. Leaving the security afforded by hugging the shoreline, we started across Frederick Sound, a twenty-mile stretch of open water between us and Admiralty Island. Even after many crossings in a small boat it was always a source of concern and apprehension to both of us. Slowing down, he stood to scan the channel ahead.

"How does it look?" I asked.

"Looks favorable," he answered. "It's flat to the south and west."

"O.K. Let's get it over with," I responded nervously.

Stu opened the throttle wide and soon Kupreanof was far behind us and I was just congratulating us on having made it halfway across in good time when I noticed the water was becoming choppy. I watched in dismay; another half hour and we would have been across. Within ten minutes more waves were building and Stu had to lessen speed and change course so as to head into the waves instead of taking them broadside. I could see the worried look on his face as he slowed down even more, maneuvering the boat to rise and fall with the waves. There were white caps as far as we could see; the sky had darkened threateningly and it was beginning to rain. We were too far across to go back, we had to go on.

Anxiously I watched the outline of Admiralty Island and when I could distinguish the individual forms of trees instead of just a dark mass, I knew we didn't have much farther to go. My legs and arms ached from bracing against the floor and sides of the boat. It was at times like this that I wondered why I had left go the storm kicked up again, forcing us to duck behind the Carroll Islands. We went ashore; Stu built a small fire and brewed fresh coffee while I opened a can of pork and beans. Turning on the short-wave channel of our portable radio we listened to Duke Short on the mailboat giving his locations but we couldn't transmit to him, our small boat not being equipped with a ship-to-shore radio.

"I don't see any eagles in the trees," Stu observed. "Evidently nothing around here for them to eat." The fire had gone out and I had turned the radio off to conserve the batteries.

"There's something moving over there in the rocks," I said pointing across the little harbor. "I think it's otter."

We sat quietly and watched several sleek otter chasing each other over rocks and driftwood and finally into the water and out again. The agile otters are considered the clowns of the fur-bearing animals. Two or three of the playful creatures wrestled and romped in the sand for a while then slid back into the water. While the others were playing, one swam out to the middle of the water and dove out of sight. When it reappeared it lay on its back with a small rock on its chest and grasping some kind of shellfish in one paw, it tapped the shell on the rock several times until it was able to pull the shell apart.

"There goes Duke now," Stu said in frustration after some two hours more of killing time. Hidden behind the small islands that protected the harbor, we sighted the mailboat only briefly passing by offshore, the large vessel not hampered by the squall. As he approached Tyee a half-hour later, we heard him talking to his family who lived at Warm Springs Bay, just across Chatham Straits from Tyee. Concerned when there was no sign of us as expected, he told them he would unload our freight and cover it as best he could with a tarp. To keep to his schedule it was necessary for him to continue on his route. His father, who had a trolling boat, told Duke he would cross over from Warm Springs later in the day and move our supplies into a cabin if we had not yet arrived. All of this we heard sitting safe on the beach, sorry we were unable to let them know we were all right and not far from Tyee.

"Oh dear," I wailed, "I hope the mink and otter don't find our groceries before we get there."

Late in the afternoon we were able to continue. Pappy Short came across to see if all was well with us and radioed word to the mailboat and other interested friends listening in, that we had finally gotten there. It was more than twenty-four hours since we had shoved off from Petersburg for a normally four or five hour trip.

174

Again we moved into the same cabin we had lived in when we first came to Tyee. But it definitely wasn't the same; the years of deterioration since the cannery had been abandoned were evident. Hunters or trappers had left their garbage behind and mice had taken over.

"This is about the last dirty cabin I ever want to clean up," I sputtered, close to tears.

"It's the worst ever," Stu agreed. "I'll help and tomorrow everything will look better. Remember there's a lot out there that we enjoyed that is the same."

He built a fire outside and we swept and burned the garbage. The legs on one side of the rusty stove had collapsed but this was easily fixed with bricks we found from an old chimney. Then Stu sloshed buckets of sea water over the walls and floor while I swept again.

"Now let's go for a walk until it dries then we'll heat some water and get settled," he suggested, trying to cheer me up. "Be careful where you step, the boardwalk is falling apart too."

It was depressing to see the remnants of the once well-maintained and busy little cannery village, but nature helps to hide the devastation wrought by men. Already three-foot high grass and flaming fireweed covered much of the ugliness. I picked a large bouquet of blue foxglove; the largest and prettiest bell-shaped flowers I had ever seen. Only the rotting pilings left standing in the quiet water were stark reminders of the depletion of one of Alaska's great resources. We finished our chores, quiet and thoughtful, to turn in, tired from our day.

The unmistakable honking of Canada geese awakened me in the morning. I jumped out of bed and went out on the porch to watch a pair of the large birds flying low, their powerful wings rising and dipping slowly, as they gracefully glided lower and passed beyond the head of Murder Cove and out of sight.

"Might be a local pair that nested in the meadow along the creek," Stu commented.

Were they then no longer searching? Was this 'beyond the horizon' for these magnificent birds?

"I'm hungry, how about hotcakes and ham for breakfast? I'll cut the ham," Stu's voice brought me back to earth.

For several days we scouted for signs of herring but there were no sea gulls swooping out over the water and no eagles perched on the big rock at Point Gardner. Nor could I sight one white head in the trees along the shore. After catching a few scattered herring one day we fished near the kelp patch where many times in the past we would see a silvery streak grab the

175

herring strip right at the stern of the boat. Then there would be some quick action and perhaps a fifty or sixty-pound king landed. Now there was nothing.

We watched for whales and sea lions but saw none as we tried again and again for salmon, finally catching a couple of small ones. With a halibut, which we caught in a deep gut at Point Gardner, and trout from the creek, we had enough fresh fish to eat. Wild goose tongue and asparagus were plentiful and rounded out our simple meals of fish, dehydrated potatoes or rice, biscuits or hardtack and an orange or apple while they lasted.

"Let's throw the clock away and forget about salmon. We'll just enjoy ourselves doing what we want to until our grub runs out, then we'll leave," Stu said one sunny morning.

"I'd like to go across Chatham and take a hot bath at Warm Springs," I proposed without delay. "The men will all be gone fishing but I'd like to visit with the women a little while."

The Short family lived in a large house on pilings at the head of a beautiful little harbor, and had several bathhouses with hot running water from the mineral springs. These were a favorite with the fishermen and other passing or visiting boats.

We walked up to a lake several hundred feet above sea level. The stream that flowed from the lake spilled over a bluff creating a waterfall which emptied into the saltwater bay. Reluctantly Stu stopped trout fishing in the crystal clear stream only when I insisted he had more than we needed. We enjoyed coffee and cake with Mrs. Short and her three daughters-in-law before leaving for Tyee.

The rest of our time at Tyee we loafed. On rainy days we rested and read and ate. Both being inveterate readers, we had brought along a good supply of reading material. Sometimes we sat at the window and watched the ravens wrangle over scraps from the table. Other times we climbed the hill to the muskeg, looked for wild flowers or tramped the beach. We explored other coves and beaches that we didn't have time for when the fishing was good. We were scraping the bottom of our larder and preparing to leave when a storm blew in and rough water prevented our traveling for five more days.

Late one afternoon two trollers anchored in the shelter of the harbor and the skippers came ashore in their little dinghies. When Stu invited them in for coffee I scowled at him, knowing how little was left in the coffee can. I used half the remaining grounds, hoping it would be strong enough to satisfy the typical fisherman's taste for coffee with plenty of flavor. I punched holes in the last of the canned milk and set it and a salmon can a third full of sugar on the table.

"I'm Eric and this is Olie," I heard one fellow say, briefly disposing of the introductions.

"Oh, oh, Swedes like their coffee thick," I groaned within.

"What are you doing here?" Olie asked after everyone had found a seat on an apple box or bench on the porch.

Stu explained why we came back after several years of good fishing. Then he asked, "Where are you fellows headed for?"

"We're going to Tebenkof Bay," Eric answered. "Heard some reports that the king fishing there is pretty good and soon there should be a run of silvers."

"Ever been there?" Olie asked. "It's a good place to fish."

"No, we haven't," Stu said. "I just know it's south of here forty-five or fifty miles, on Kuiu Island."

Olie told us that it was a large bay several miles across each way, dotted with many small islands and good sheltered channels where small boats could fish.

"And there's a fishbuyer's scow anchored there all season. It has a cold storage and groceries," he said.

"Hey! that sounds good!" Stu said, with a return of his old enthusiasm.

"Is there anything there to live in?" I interrupted to ask and at the same time wondering if my usually most important concern would throw a wet blanket over his rising spirits.

"No," one of the fellows answered. "There's not a building in the whole bay. What you need is a bigger boat."

After the fellows went back to their boats, Stu said, "Let's pack up what we can tonight, the wind's going down and I think we can leave in the morning."

In the morning after breakfast I cleaned up the dishes and put the last of the coffee in the thermos for the trip. A little pancake flour and a half a package of dry milk was all the groceries left.

Stu let the boat drift a minute when we crossed the waters where we had once seen so much action and wildlife. He waved his arm in a sweeping gesture. "It's like a graveyard here now, no life."

"I liked it so much here," I agreed sadly. "I sure hate to see it go to pot."

"We'll try Tebenkof Bay next year," he said eagerly. "Maybe it will be even better."

I felt a tremor in my stomach as for a moment I thought only of another move. But wasn't that what I wanted — to see more of this great northland? There would be more wilderness, new

177

adventures, new islands and coves to explore and I had never seen a fishbuyer's scow. There might be a woman on the scow and maybe one on some of the trolling boats that come in to sell their catches. I turned to Stu with a smile.

"I'm getting excited already. I want to see Tebenkof Bay." Then I added, "But *where* will we live?"

"We'll think of something, don't worry," he said squeezing my hand. "Now let's get going."

23

Penthouse in Tebenkof Bay

"Time to get at the fishing," my husband announced one morning standing at the open door of our tenthouse in Tebenkof Bay.

"If we make this shack too comfortable you won't want to leave it and I'll lose my fishing partner. Can't spoil you now."

With that he proceeded to load the fishing gear into our new nineteen-foot sportfishing boat that we had bought in Portland, Oregon a year before. The tri-hulled craft, a factory-named Thunderbird, was built wide of beam, deep and roomy, and was convenient for fishing as well as being a good sea boat. With an adjustable canvas canopy, a mattress and sleeping bags under the decking in the bow, and a large water-tight can of provisions we could stay aboard comfortably overnight or even for several days. Although our faithful little sixteen-foot Reinall was a good sea craft, it was much less boat and I had often grasped the side tensely as we bounced in turbulent waters. I felt much more secure in the new one and could easily stand upright in it when traveling.

We had fished one summer off the coast of Oregon, thinking we would take advantage of better weather and water conditions. But many mornings there was heavy fog until noon or after and almost every day about noontime a stubborn breeze from the north made fishing with the sports-size boats precarious and the bar crossing dangerous. The constant swells that often made both of us seasick were a complete and unpleasant surprise because neither one of us was ever seasick in the roughest of water in Alaska. Neither could we fish anchored, nor by using the same procedures as up north. And I was terrified of crossing the bar

179

which it is necessary to do from any harbor on the Oregon coast. The swells can pile up the waves on the bar in a short time, creating huge combers where boats are lost almost every year. Before the season was over I point blank refused to make one more crossing.

"Let's chuck the whole thing and go back home," Stu said in disgust. I needed no prodding.

So now we were in Tebenkof Bay. Having loaded our boat and pickup with supplies in April, we trailered the boat over the Cariboo Trail in British Columbia to Prince Rupert. There we wheeled aboard a ferry for Petersburg. The passenger steamboats had gone out of business due to the overwhelming use of plane service and were replaced by diesel-powered ferryboats. Although providing much less luxury and service, they had proved to be more economical and faster, with no layovers in the cities.

Miles of uninhabited wilderness stretched in either direction from Tebenkof Bay along Chatham Straits on the west coast of Kuiu Island. Within the large bay, which was several miles long, scattered groups of small densely wooded islands offered protected waters for small boats. A fish-buyer scow, anchored in Explorer Basin, a natural harbor deep in the bay, was equipped with a power plant, cold storage and a good supply of groceries and fishing gear. Unlike the buyer in Angoon who hauled his own loads to the city, the iced fish on the scow in Tebenkof was loaded onto a packer boat about once a week and delivered to the cold storage in town. On the second floor of the scow were living quarters for Orwan and Barbara Simpson, the capable and friendly operators of the business. A mail plane stopped once a week. Often there were thirty or forty trolling boats anchored in the harbor at night.

It was here on the beach in Explorer Basin, conveniently close to the scow, that we set up camp. What groceries and supplies we couldn't bring out in our own boat we had put aboard the fish packer in Petersburg. Although I had bought a big supply of staple groceries there, I wasn't too concerned about the quantity, knowing there was a small store on the scow and that I'd have the opportunity to send in orders with the packer. One of the especially hard-to-get items that we had brought with us from Portland was eight dozen fresh eggs which I had packed carefully and guarded jealously all the way.

"Be careful of my eggs," I admonished Stu a dozen times a day all the way up the highway. The eggs that reach Alaska have always been notoriously unfresh. In fact, the old-timers claimed they couldn't stand "those fresh eggs they feed you outside."

Included in our supplies from Portland were several lengths of garden hose and a large sheet of heavy duty plastic. A short distance above the beach Stu stretched a heavy wire between two large hemlock trees, split a length of hose to cover the wire, then spread the plastic sheet over the hose to form a large tent. We weighted down the bottom edges of the plastic all around with rocks carried up from the beach. After setting up an oil drum stove and two folding cots, we moved in. I used a two-burner Coleman camp stove for cooking. It was faster and much of the time in the summer we didn't need heat from the big stove.

"How do you like that?" Stu asked, surveying his see-through construction. Then added, "The only pent-house in Tebenkof Bay!"

"It's great," I assured him. Then the ever-practical house-wife added "all we need is running water."

"That's easy," he responded to my surprise, "I'll use the other hose to run the spring water right to your door."

His water system was a source of amazement to our native friends who had camps on the beach too, but had never thought of doing anything but pack water in a bucket. Because of the excessive rain, camps along the beach were few. Most fishermen lived on their boats if at all possible but sometimes a few young people from the city would put up tents for a summer's fishing. The natives, when fishing away from their own village, made simple rough camps that served the most basic needs, and usually cooked outside over a fire. Some used small tents and others made shelters under the big trees from driftwood and branches. Besides supplementing the limited space on their small crafts, it gave them freedom to hunt, pick berries or smoke fish, all a part of their life.

After prowling through the abandoned herring processing plant at Washington Bay ten or fifteen miles up the coast, we returned with a couple of chairs, a folding table and surprisingly, a small Oriental rug. Although well-worn, the latter added considerably to our comfort when spread over the dirt floor. My prize find was a good toilet seat, a big improvement over the jagged-cut hole in a big fish box set back in a clump of trees. Stretching a piece of plastic between branches to form a roof, I confided to a curious raven perched in a nearby tree, "Happiness is a dry toilet seat."

This was without doubt the most bizarre home we had lived in since coming to Alaska. Always before we'd had a solid roof over our heads. Now, more than once after a rainy night, I awoke to see over my head a big dip in the plastic roof, holding at least a bucket full of water. Reaching up I gingerly pushed up the plastic to let the water run off. But in spite of a few flaws it really was a cozy camp where we enjoyed the company of the Simpsons and other friends in the rare moments they found to get away from work.

We became acquainted with a middle-aged native couple, Willy and Martha, who were camped not far from us. They often came for coffee after a cold rainy day and sat warming themselves by our oil-drum stove.

So much room in here, so big," Martha said on their first visit, "light too."

"And warm," Willy added with hands stretched over the stove.

"You make comfortable camp," she said, indicating the worn rug, chairs and running water at the door. A kettle of beans simmered on the top of the stove.

"You build a place for boat?" Willy asked in astonishment when they discovered the float in front of our camp. Stu had built the float from drift boards and logs and anchored it in water deep enough to keep the boat afloat at the lowest tide. Instead of leaving the boat on the beach where it would need to be watched and moved with the tide changes, as was necessary for most campers, we could safely moor it to the float. With logs fastened together we also had a walkway from the float to the shore.

"When we're through fishing we'll leave the camp as is," Stu told our friends. "Use it if you want to."

"Good," the native answered. "We don't know yet how long we stay."

"You come see us when you come to Petersburg," Martha said.

"We'd like to," I assured her.

Our new friends showed us some of their favorite fishing spots and Stu showed them how to jig for herring with a string of hooks. We later learned that when we left early one morning in late summer, we had hardly disappeared around the bend before the native Indians moved into our camp but we never knew if it was our friends.

At night the glistening lights of the large scow and fishing boats, the effect doubled by the reflections in the water, looked like a tiny glittering city, bravely pushing back the darkness of the surrounding wilderness. Often from inside our plastic home we watched as the lights went out one by one, leaving only the small foremast light above each boat, tiny sentinels on watch over the sleeping harbor.

182

After a few weeks of fishing in Tebenkof Bay we found a couple of favorite spots and returned to them regularly. One was just outside Mailboat Pass, a passageway between two islands. The tides boiling through the narrow channel created currents that formed an eddy in a bight along the south shore of the pass. One evening after fishing quite late it was so balmy and peaceful we decided to anchor in a pretty little cove for the night.

"It will be quiet sleeping here," Stu decided, "and we can get an early start in the morning."

We had settled into our sleeping bags under the decking in the bow of the boat and I was just about asleep when a wolf howled from a nearby bluff, one lonely spine-tingling howl. I snuggled deeper. The next thing I knew it was daylight and Stu was pulling the anchor.

"Aren't we going to eat breakfast first?" I asked sleepily.

"Come on, get out of the sack," he replied. "We'll anchor in the bight by Mailboat Pass, then I can hang a line over while you stir up the hotcakes." Grudgingly I crawled out, dressed and washed my face in a basin of cold water as we glided slowly between the islands.

It was a delightful morning, fresh and invigorating with the fragrance of salt water and evergreen trees. I spied a mother duck in the shadows close to shore with fourteen little ones trailing behind her in single file. Several ravens argued over some sort of scrap on the beach, hopping around sideways in their comical manner.

"There's herring here," Stu commented, pointing to a bald eagle swooping swiftly down over the water making an unsuccessful attempt to grasp a herring in its talons.

A few minutes later, anchored just inside the eddy, my impatient fisherman cast a line out into the current and propped his pole against the boat. I perked the coffee on the one-burner gas stove and using the large tin can on which our food rested I started mixing hotcake batter.

"How about a cup of Java?" Stu asked, reaching for a mug. Then, 'Wham!' his pole jerked downward and the reel unwound with a screech. Grabbing his pole he yelled, "Throw the buoy over!" We didn't dare try to land a salmon so close to shore because the line would get tangled in the kelp patch. In my hurry to get going, I started the boat moving with a series of jerks that upset the coffee pot; the dishes and hotcake batter all crashed to the floor, and in a few minutes a forty-eight pound salmon was dumped right in the middle of it all.

"Sorry about that," Stu grinned.

"You look like it," I muttered.

Back at the buoy he helped me clean up the mess. The dishes were plastic so they weren't damaged but the batter was a complete loss. Again he dropped a bait into the water in spite of my strong protest.

"I'm getting hungry, fishing can wait a while," I complained.

I mixed more batter, placed the gas stove on the floor this time, heated the griddle, ladled out four hotcakes and had just flipped them over when Stu got another strike.

"I think it's a small one," he said. "Let's try and get it in without moving the boat." After landing it I turned and pointed to the griddle still on the stove.

"There's your breakfast." The hotcakes were burned crisp, the edges curled up.

"But we're making money," Stu rationalized. I knew the fun he was having far outweighed the value of a few dollars, more or less.

"Oh, all right," he added amiably, "I won't fish until we've had breakfast."

Again I heated the coffee and we both enjoyed a long delayed cup while the griddle reheated.

"Feel better now?" he grinned. Beginning to relax, I managed a smile, nodded and dipped out four more hotcakes. Suddenly there was an eruption in the water not more than fifty feet away!

"What the hell!" Stu blurted and we both jumped to our feet to see two big whales lunge halfway out of the water, their huge mouths gaping wide, their powerful flippers violently churning the water. Quickly Stu jumped forward and turned on the motor. A frightened "My gosh!" was all I could get out. I did think to turn off the gas stove.

Breathlessly I saw the forty-ton creatures coming closer, still threshing the water. Then at the sound of the motor they made a right-angle turn and as they partially submerged, the barnacles clinging to their blotchy black hides were plainly visible. The turbulent waves created by their acrobatics rocked the boat about, causing things to roll and slide back and forth on the floor. I saw the hotcakes slide by at least twice.

Bracing against the side of the boat we watched the whales slowly move farther away, one trailing the other by half a length. They may have been feeding on plankton or tiny newly-hatched tom cod which we had seen in the water. Then in a graceful move they started a dive, their backs arching. As they turned downward, their huge tails slid out of the water, poised for a moment ten feet in the air, then slapped the water with a resounding blast just before disappearing beneath the surface. It would certainly have spelled disaster for us if we had been within range of those powerful tails.

With a big sigh of relief I turned and picked up the griddle from the floor. The hotcakes were half-baked, the tops white with well defined bubble holes. We looked at each other and laughed as I tossed them overboard.

"Let's go to the penthouse and have breakfast in peace," my over-zealous fisherman conceded.

Several days later we anchored in Happy Cove when the water became sloppy in the channel where we had been fishing. Located on the east shore of the Bay, the circular little harbor bordered with a heavy growth of trees was one of my favorite hideaways.

"Shall we anchor and rest awhile?" I suggested. "No use taking a beating in this choppy water."

The water in the cove was alive with herring, feeding and flipping. As I leaned back in my seat, I became aware of a low chirping.

"Sounds like eagles," I said, sitting up.

"It is," Stu answered. "Look in the trees."

"Oh, there's lots of them," I exclaimed, observing first the many white heads of the adult bald eagles, and then looking more closely, to the younger ones, not yet white.

"They were probably fishing for herring," Stu said, "and we disturbed them. Let's keep real still and see what happens."

We sat perfectly quiet for perhaps fifteen minutes before one of the big birds finally flew out over the water, circled, then quickly swooped down in a vain attempt to pick a herring out of the water with its sharp talons. Then one after another, from all sides of the cove they began to glide swiftly down, wings outstretched, often a five or six foot span. Then they soared upward to perch on a limb before trying again.

We noted that only about once in five attempts did an eagle rise clutching a wriggling herring in its claws. We watched, fascinated, for an hour. Sometimes one passed within a few feet of us, seemingly convinced that this stationary object was no hazard. But the moment we made a movement in the boat, all activity stopped and they watched us from the treetops.

We fished in Tebenkof Bay for two summers and made the one-hundred mile trip to and from Petersburg twice each year in our boat. Just once in the four trips were we stormbound overnight. That was near Kake on Kupreanof Island.

A breeze ruffled the water after we left Petersburg but it didn't slow us down until we were near the north-end of the island when it became quite rough and we could see white water in the distance.

"It doesn't look very good along these rocks," Stu said, looking for a sheltered nook to duck into.

The wind and rain increased in intensity when we turned west and the deepening waves slowed us to a crawl.

"Why not follow those boats," I said anxiously, pointing to several small native boats, all going in the same direction. Just then one of the fellows in the boat nearest us motioned for us to follow. A few minutes later we were in calm water in a small, nearly landlocked harbor, where we spent a comfortable night in our bed under the decking. Even the rain beating on the deck less than two feet above our heads didn't keep me awake.

At the end of the season we put the boat in storage in Petersburg and called our native friends while waiting for the ferry. They showed us around the shrimp cannery where they both worked whenever there was enough shrimp harvested to process. Willy was foreman. He and his wife were hard workers, steady and dependable and they never lacked employment. They were active members of a church in town and lived in one of the older houses, a two-storey well-built and nicely-kept home.

By the late sixties we were spending more winters outside, now more commonly referred to as the lower forty-eight. Although the Alaskan cities now boasted supermarkets and many of the other advantages and frills of their southern counterparts, conditions in the wilderness areas remained much the same as when we first saw it. True, plane service and radio communication was more easily accessible, but the challenge of matching wits with the quirks of nature never changed.

By the end of a rainy fishing season, Stu was now beginning to hanker for the sunshine and freedom from shoveling snow, heavy boots and layers of wool clothing. I admit that comfort in the form of hot showers and automatic washers was more attractive each year. But I also missed the northern winters, the nights white and sparkling beneath brilliant stars, the flamboyant northern lights, snow brushing my cheeks and a cozy fire on a stormy day.

"I would like to come back a couple of summers yet," Stu said as we walked back through the boat harbor, "but I don't think we can make a living at this much longer."

"I wish we could find some place to fish where there's a

house to live in," I said.

"Do you remember the Simpsons told us what a pretty place Saginaw Bay is?" he asked.

"Yes. Didn't they have the scow anchored in there one summer?" I recalled. "Must be salmon there."

"And they said there's some empty buildings there too," Stu said, getting more enthusiastic all the time. "What do you say we go there next summer if we can rent one to live in?"

"Okay, but I want to be sure of a place to live before we go this time," I said, a bit uneasy about another move into an unknown situation. "It does sound interesting," I admitted after a few minutes. "Barbara Simpson did say there are spectacular cliffs and fossils on the beaches. There will be new nooks and crannies to explore."

I began to feel the old wilderness challenge. Hooking my arm in Stu's, I grinned up at him. "Yeah, let's go, I'm anxious to see it."

24

Frustration

A slightly built man with stooped shoulders stood waiting as we rounded a huge rock a short distance off shore and minutes later eased the boat alongside a float in Saginaw Bay.

"I'm Mac Hammer," he said. "I got your message and your cabin is ready for you." I wondered if a man's idea of a clean cabin was the same as mine. I breathed a sigh of relief when he added, "My wife fixed it up yesterday before she went to Kake."

"Nice place here," Stu said as he shook hands with the old man.

"Come on, I'll show you your cabin, then you can unload." Leading the way, Mac stepped agilely along a large floating log to the beach while I held my breath, expecting the log to roll over any moment. Not until I saw that one end rested on the beach would I venture across.

We went up the beach to a badly worn boardwalk that connected several buildings in varying states of disrepair. They were all that remained of a herring saltery that had closed down sometime in the twenties. Hundreds of barrels of herring had been salted down and shipped to outside markets, mostly in the eastern states.

"This is yours," Mac said, opening the door of a one-room, solidly built cabin. "It was used for a meat house and it's well-insulated. There are beds and mattresses in that bunk house over there. Help yourself."

Mac and his wife Lois, lived in the only real house, a four-room dwelling with a bath, which no doubt had been the home of the top man, whether he was owner, superintendent or manager. The company had hired Mac as watchman for many years and when the business was abandoned he acquired the buildings as compensation for wages. He was a friendly gray-haired fellow with a wealth of stories to tell and welcomed company because he loved to talk. In the summer Lois worked in the general store in Kake, an Indian village about twenty miles to the east.

"What do you do all winter?" Stu asked later that evening while we sat on an old bench on the boardwalk. A sudden breeze sent a flurry of ripples across the water.

"Wife and I trap wolves part of the time. We don't have to go far from the house or beach, they come in close. Sometimes we see one on the path over there by the old warehouse," he told us. "My wife has a closet full of pelts, she'll show you next time she's home."

"Let's go explore the fishing prospects," Stu said the next day after we had browsed through the two-storey bunkhouse and a large warehouse full of old nets, stoves, bear and wolf traps and other reminders of a bustling enterprise of the past. Many of the pilings under the warehouse were almost destroyed by teredos, a worm-like mollusk that will bore into any kind of wood under water. Clam shells and rocks in the shape of crude tools could be seen where the bank had eroded — signs that this had probably been the site of an Indian village over a hundred years earlier.

"When my wife comes home she'll take you out to hunt fossils," Mac promised. "She knows where to find them."

"How does she go to Kake?" I asked.

"Sometimes she catches a ride with a fisherman going that way. Otherwise I radio in and the plane from Petersburg stops for her," he replied.

"What a striking setting," I remarked as we slowly cruised along the shore rimmed with sheer cliffs rising from deep water. On the top of the cliffs grew the lush evergreen forest typical of southeastern Alaska. The opposite shore was also heavily wooded, as were numerous small islands scattered through Saginaw Bay. Dark patches of kelp in several places close to shore indicated shallow water.

"Looks fishy here," Stu said when we reached the entrance to the bay. A large kelp bed extended from a rocky point and we saw a few herring flipping in water stirred by small rip-tides from the currents in Frederick Sound.

"Just as well catch a few herring and start fishing as long as we're here," he said casually, reaching for his jigging pole. I had long suspected that Stu enjoyed jigging for herring almost as much as fishing for salmon. At times when I insisted we had plenty of bait and that he could now fish for salmon which after all, meant our bread and butter, he would cheerfully agree saying, "Okay, Okay, just one more cast."

Stu told me that Ray Bell who owned the store at Kake had a big boat that he used to haul supplies and that he also bought fish. "He'll bring us ice once a week and pick up our fish when he goes to Petersburg."

"How will he know we're here?" I asked.

"Mac said he'd call him on the radio," Stu replied. "Besides, almost everyone has a ship to shore radio on their boat now and I'll bet everyone within a hundred miles already knows we're here."

For several weeks the fishing was fair and we kept at it quite steady so as to make it pay for the buyer to travel the extra miles to pick up our salmon. Because of the decreasing king runs we were satisfied now to catch five or six good-sized fish a day. With the price increase we could still make expenses.

On stormy days, during unfavorable tides or when we were just plain tired of fishing, we walked the beach or explored coves and channels at the head of the bay. Mac showed us where to sink the crab pot. When several crabs had been trapped we transferred them to a permanent pot tied to the end of the float so anytime we felt the urge for a crab feed there were live ones available.

Twice during the summer we made the twenty-mile trip to Kake for mail and groceries. We traveled through waters made precarious by rocks and reefs, many of which were submerged during the higher tides.

"Just line up between the Kake cannery smokestack at your back, and the first Keku island ahead of you, and you'll be all right," Wayne Short advised. We were always relieved to turn again into the sheltered waters of Saginaw Bay.

"Let's quit for the day and go beachcombing," I suggested hopefully early one afternoon. "Not much doing anyway."

"Can't make any money that way," Stu grumbled, putting a fresh bait on his hook. Just then I was more interested in thumbing through the small tide book that we always carried with us. Each leaf represented a month and was dog-eared in turn. More and more often when nearing the end of a summer I would sneak a look to see how many more leafs there were to dog-ear before we could hang up the fishing poles for another season.

The fishing had been slow for several days but today it was even more so. In the past two hours I had caught only three small salmon while Stu had missed several strikes. Even though we had developed a method of efficient team-work, we had never lost the

190

sense of exciting sport and challenge there was in battling the big kings with our light gear. The suspense never ended until the salmon was safely inside the boat. Many times I was so tired I almost gave up before we finally hauled in a big one, but today I was tired without much of a battle.

The foremost purpose was to make the day's fishing pay off, so we worked together without rivalry. After all my husband was the real fisherman. I didn't know one end of a fish from the other until I met him. However we each had our own pole and played our own strike but both were happy when the salmon was landed.

Nevertheless it was frustrating for one to have a streak of bad luck, consistently losing strikes or not even getting a nibble while the other hauled in one fish after the other. It didn't bother me much when I had the off days; it was a good excuse to suggest going beachcombing. When Stu, the expert, experienced the exasperating unlucky days I could definitely sense the deterioration of his normally good disposition.

"Something's wrong with my reel," he growled. Then, "My hook must be dull." Soon the complaints were directed at me. "Better change your bait."

"Nothing doing anyway," I responded watching the flight of three small ducks, all black except for bright red web feet stretched out behind like little red flags.

I was hoping his luck would change and his disposition along with it. It had been an exasperating afternoon and I was weary anyway. After a long season suddenly I was tired of fishing, of the slimy herring, of the smell of fish-guts, of the scratchy long johns and of the long hours squirming on the hard boat seat. Having just lost my bait to a scrap fish I rebelled at cutting even one more stinky herring, so I quietly let my line back into the water without a bait. Now if a salmon came along it would have to take Stu's bait.

Making myself as comfortable as possible by leaning back against the side of the boat, I continued to go through the motions of fishing, stripping the line in part way then letting it back, being careful not to bring it up far enough so Stu could see there was no bait on the hook. He was fishing diligently, changing baits, trying different depths, and all the while prodding me with a steady stream of advice. "See if your bait's working."

"It's O.K.," I replied.

After a few minutes, "Better see if your hook is sharp."

"Ah-huh," I responded listlessly.

Then, "The salmon must be deep, let out more line."

No comment.

191

After strong mutterings over catching several scrap fish he spoke a bit more hopefully, "I see herring around the boat, should get a good strike any time." Again, "Don't just sit there, check your bait." Grudgingly I slowly reeled in as if to check but let the line down again, still baitless. I was determined my frustrated man was going to make the next catch. I was tired of his growling so I settled back holding my pole. Out of habit I kept a sensitive finger lightly touching the line.

I watched some bald-headed eagles in the trees along shore. They never ceased to fascinate me, perched in regal dignity or swooping down over the water, their majestic wings spread wide. I learnt they do not attain the white feathers on the head and tail until seven years old. Both male and female build the nest, sit on the eggs and feed the young ones. I thought of the previous summer in Tebenkof Bay when on the way to and from fishing we daily watched a pair of nesting eagles. Intently we had followed their activities from the time we first noticed them carrying sticks, which looked to be from six inches to two feet long, to the top of a large hemlock tree near the edge of a bluff overlooking the water. Either the nest was over half finished or they were repairing the old one when we first saw them; eagles come back to the same nest year after year. They had chosen well as the top of the tree had broken off almost even with large wide-spread branches providing an ideal site for a nest. Each day the nest grew larger until it looked at least six or seven feet across and over two feet deep.

Finally the huge nest seemed to be finished and for a long time we saw only one eagle at a time. We didn't know how long it would be before the female finished laying eggs or how many there might be. Finally they were taking turns staying on the nest and we waited and watched anxiously for signs of hatching. It must have been six or seven weeks from the time we guessed the eggs were laid until we heard new chirping sounds and days later we occasionally caught sight of a small fluffy head above the top of the nest. More and more we heard the clamoring when the parent birds brought feed to the young but they were almost full grown before we saw the two fledglings perching, wobbly and uncertain, on the edge of the nest. For many days they flapped, stretched and exercised their wings and seemed to have a voracious appetite. Then one day the adult eagles, by flying back and forth short distances from the nest, wheedled and coaxed the young into making their first floundering flights.

My eyes moved across the straits where the craggy, permanently snow-covered mountain peaks on Baranof Island loomed

192

against a background of blue sky and white billowy clouds. I smiled as I recalled the winter we were in southern California visiting friends who wanted to treat us with a trip to Big Bear to see the snow.

Resting comfortably in the warm sun I was feeling quite drowsy when Stu's voice roused me. "Time you changed your bait." Before I had time to answer I felt a succession of tiny tugs on my line. I sat up, realizing that a herring must have mistaken the shiny unbaited hook for shrimp spawn and had managed to hook itself.

"I must have a small scrap," I said casually and started to reel in my line.

"It's no wonder, with your bait just hanging there. Keep it moving," Stu grumbled impatiently.

'At least we'll have fresh bait, grouchy,' I thought. I could still feel the little jerks on the line as the herring tried to free itself.

All of a sudden the pole jerked down hard and the reel started humming while the line unwound speedily. Getting a better grip on the pole, I stood up just as a large salmon leaped clear of the water a 100 feet from us. Incredulous, I yelled, "That's mine!"

"Well, I know it," Stu responded testily, no doubt wondering why I was so surprised — after all, we hooked salmon every day.

"Hold your pole higher," he ordered, throwing the anchor buoy overboard. Soon we landed a nice king, the biggest of the day.

"Sometimes you can't lose," I muttered under my breath, almost afraid to look at my disgruntled fisherman. But he looked at me while a big grin spread over his face. "I give up. Let's go beachcombing."

25

Visitors in Saginaw Bay

The small shuttle plane from Sitka circled and landed on a narrow strip of smooth water between the rocky shore and a small island. It was piloted by one of the renowned bush pilots of Alaska; men who went out of their way to deliver a puppy to the little boy of an isolated family; who waited patiently for a prescription to be filled; who flew late into the night to bring help to an accident victim; who tried desperately to deliver parcels or a bottle of cheer in time for Christmas and perhaps spent their own Christmas making it a less lonely day for others miles from family or friends.

As the plane taxied alongside the float where we stood, Stu and I waited eagerly to greet our friends, Kenneth and Audrey Matzen from Seattle, whom we had met years ago in Mazatlan, Mexico. Visitors from the States were a rare treat in isolated Saginaw Bay, and because most of our chance callers were men, I was tickled to have Audrey to visit with for two whole weeks.

"Watch your step," Stu warned picking up a suitcase and leading the way from the float to shore, a precarious walk on floating logs nailed together with scraps of old boards.

"Let's have coffee and hear the latest news before we show Audrey and Kenny to their cabin," I suggested.

"Yes, they may need a bracer when they see their cottage," Stu said with a grin while emphasizing 'cottage'.

"Mac, want you to meet our friends from the south," Stu said when we passed his house.

"Here's today's paper," Kenny offered.

"We don't often get one that fresh," Mac responded smiling.

While having coffee in our cabin, Audrey carefully removed

194

packed fruit from a suitcase — peaches, cantaloupe, and plums — a real treat.

"Where do we park our sleeping bags?" Kenny asked impatiently, pushing his chair back. "And when do we start fishing?"

"Come on," Stu said, leading the way to the end of the board-walk, then along the rocky beach a short distance and finally through grass three feet high to an unpainted one-room cabin with broken down steps. A remnant of the saltery days, it was the only usable one left. Inside were two folding cots with mattresses that Stu had brought over from the bunkhouse, a couple of old chairs, a bench with a tin basin, a water bucket and a coal oil lamp. Half of a broken mirror hung on the wall.

"You'll hardly need the lamp," I assured our guests, "It's light most of the night now."

"It's a bucket camp," Stu said with mock seriousness, pointing to the roof, through which daylight showed in various cracks. "If it rains you hang buckets under the drips."

Audrey stood staring dubiously at the roof but the apprehension quickly left her face when I gestured towards the window.

"Just look at the view, Audrey, never mind the roof. Maybe it won't rain." One window faced the blue water of Saginaw Bay, a huge bare rock offshore at the foot of a sheer bluff and two small forested islands.

"The heck with the buckets, everything is great! Let's get unpacked," Kenny interrupted. The rough hewn surroundings in no way dampened the enthusiasm of either.

I prepared lunch while Stu showed our friends his smoke-house, the shelves filled with thick juicy chunks of kippered salmon done to a golden brown. No one needed a second invitation to help himself.

"Old Mac is going to have a lot of help now keeping the fire going," Stu grinned. We would often see Mac come from the direction of the smokehouse smacking his lips. "Just fixing the fire," he explained with a smile.

"Help yourself whenever you want to, Mac," Stu had told the likeable old fellow who was always accommodating and anxious to please. He was not physically able to sit out in a boat or handle a fishing pole any longer but he offered to keep the fire going in the smokehouse while we fished.

"There will be plenty of kipper for all of us," Stu assured him. "I'm mighty glad to get to use your big smokehouse."

The days were filled with activity: fishing, setting crab pots, digging clams, canning salmon, picking salmon berries and beachcombing. Every day Audrey and I gathered wild asparagus from the thick clumps that grew in abundance along the beach. We experimented with it, preparing it raw, steamed, cooked or fried and liked it about as well one way as another.

At every meal there were decisions to make. What should we eat? Grilled salmon or baked halibut? Kippered salmon or cracked crabs? Butter clams or delicious "beer bits"? Dessert might be the large succulent salmonberries or wild blueberry pie. Mac was usually waiting on the float to meet us when we came in from fishing and we often asked him to have dinner with us. He would just about beat us home, usually stopping in his storehouse to bring along a can of fruit.

Because of the steadily decreasing king salmon runs, Stu and I no longer depended on the fishing but had an alternate income from a tree farm in Oregon which we had bought on one of our trips south. We could harvest the Christmas trees in the winter and go to Alaska in the summer, satisfied to make expenses for the season while enjoying more leisure. This was the last year that we bought a commercial license, paying $109. for it. The first one we bought had cost one dollar.

One afternoon the fishing was slow and we were lazily enjoying the warm sunny day, our lines hanging in the water, when Audrey said, "I'm tired of losing bait to the scrap fish, I'm going to try fly fishing."

"You can't catch a salmon with a fly," the men laughed.

"I can have fun trying," she retorted. Taking her pole she stood on the forward deck of the boat, casting out and ignoring the men's ribbing.

"Do you hear that low chirping? What kind of birds are they?" Kenny asked during a lull in the conversation.

"It's those bald eagles," Stu replied, pointing towards shore where several of the huge birds known for their deadly hunting instincts, perched high in the trees, alert and waiting with unflagging patience to swoop down on some small victim.

"I can't believe it," Kenny exclaimed, "You wouldn't think that pleasant chirping could come from a bird like that."

We agreed it seemed more like the sounds of small birds but assured him the innocent twitter could quickly change to angry and frenzied shrieks.

"I've got something!" Audrey suddenly shouted. "It's a salmon!"

"Can't be, not on a fly!" the men exclaimed, jumping to their feet.

"But it is!" she insisted, struggling with the jerking pole and

196

unwinding reel, all the time receiving a barrage of unasked-for advice.

"Hold your pole higher!" "Let it run!" "Reel it in!" "Watch the slack!"

Soon she maneuvered it in close, Stu slipped the net under it and dropped a sixteen-pound dog salmon at her feet.

"So I can't catch a salmon on a fly?" she mocked proudly.

"You're the champion fly fisherman. I've never heard of anyone ever catching a salmon on a fly," Stu assured her.

"What kind is it?" Audrey asked, "doesn't look like a king."

"It's a dog salmon, called that because of its canine-like teeth that develop on the journey to its spawning grounds," Stu explained. "The real name is chum and yours is an unusually big one. These go to the cannery and fresh fish market."

"Don't they can king salmon?" Kenny asked.

"Oh no. Kings are much too expensive for canning." And Stu went on to explain how the kings are split and salted in 800 pound terses, shipped mostly to the east coast cities, processed and sold on the markets like bacon.

"Chums, pinks (humpies) and sockeye are the species of salmon caught with seine nets for the canneries," he told them. "Silvers are mainly sold for the fresh fish market. These species never get large like the king."

The following day we went into Halleck Harbor to pick salmonberries. The terrain was less rugged here and berry bushes covered several acres. Audrey and I started picking together but soon wandered apart. After a while I heard a rustle on the other side of a large clump of bushes where I was picking and thinking it was Audrey, I made some comment. Hearing no answer I spoke louder. Just as she replied from some distance away and behind me, there was a crash on the other side of my bush and I got a frightened glimpse of the rear end of a black bear disappearing into the brush. I hastily retreated and the two of us stayed together, talking loudly until our pails were filled with large, luscious red and yellow berries.

Bears were not such a hazard here since there were no brownies on Kuiu Island, only blacks. Nevertheless I have a healthy respect for them too, although they are not as dangerous. Black bear will not stay in the same areas as the more aggressive brownies.

The weather held unusually good those weeks for southeastern Alaska. The bucket camp remained dry. We cooked and ate in our one-room cabin, sometimes five of us, including Mac. Audrey and I managed on the two-burner Coleman stove by shifting kettles and double decking. We used the oven of Mac's kitchen range once in a while for baking. There was a small oil-burning heating stove when needed. Aside from several choices of seafood our meals were simple but adequate; de-hydrated potatoes or rice, hard tack or biscuits, wild asparagus or a store can of vegetables and wild berries. Everyone was in a jolly frame of mine. The Matzens even enjoyed the rough improvising which was a daily part of life in the north which Stu and I had long since taken for granted. No one lost weight.

When Mac's wife came home for a few days she showed us where to find petrified fossils on the beach. There were clam shells imbedded in rocks and chunks of clay or mud full of various sea worms and other sea animal life, all petrified — also cone-shaped coral and things we couldn't identify.

We canned several cases of salmon, kept the smokehouse busy and sold the surplus to the fishpacker who came by once a week bringing us ice for a large fish box which the men had built on the float. To better insulate it, we stuffed the double walls with moss gathered from the dense woods.

One week we had a little more excitement than usual. Stu hooked an unusually heavy strike and thought for the first forty-five minutes it was a salmon or big halibut although its actions were typical of neither.

"If this is a salmon it's the granddaddy of them all," he yelled as Kenny maneuvered the boat, trying to follow the speedy and powerful swimmer at the end of the line. From his position in the stern Kenny couldn't see which way the strange fish was traveling and was hard put to follow the frantically shouted orders of the three of us.

"Turn this way!"

"Faster! Faster!"

Then, "The other way, hurry!"

"Step on it!" Stu yelled. "Not much line left on the reel."

"What is it? Can you see it?" Audrey asked a little later, leaning over the edge of the boat.

"Can't see it yet but we're gaining on it now and it's near the surface," Stu replied. "If it's a salmon it's a hell-uv-a big one," he added, wishful thinking evident on his ruddy face. "But —," and he left the suggestion of doubt unfinished.

We were out of the bay and into Frederick Sound before Stu motioned Kenny to slow up. Watching tensely we soon made out a large dark form near the bow of the boat still moving strongly.

"It's a damn shark!" Stu exploded, thoroughly disgusted. "At least ten feet long."

I held his pole while he shot it three times with the big rifle. The bullet holes visible on the dark hide never slowed it down so Stu broke his line and let the monster go.

Then a few days later when Kenny hooked a king, he was soon aware it was the biggest salmon he had ever battled. Now he was the target of a steady stream of advice. His face displayed anxiety, hope and tension in turn, as the unyielding fish made repeated runs, circled the boat and leaped clear of the water.

"He's gone," Stu teased. Then, "Just as well cut it loose, you'll never land him."

"The hell I won't!" Kenny snapped back.

After a half-hour struggle he boated a beautiful forty-five pound king, its silvery skin glistening in the sunlight.

"What a fighter!" Kenny gasped, trembling with excitement and happiness. "That's by far the largest salmon I've ever caught." Impulsively he kissed the women. Audrey and I maintain he kissed Stu too, which they both vehemently deny.

"I'm satisfied. My trip is complete," Kenny smiled as we headed for camp.

26

Mixed Emotions

The jangling of the alarm clock near my head jarred me awake. My husband stirred, grunted, then with a big sigh turned his back on the noise. I turned my head to glance across the room and out the uncurtained window hoping it was still dark so I could postpone leaving the comfort of the bed a few minutes. But my eyes opened wide. The sky was ablaze with rays from a red sun not yet visible above the tree tops.

"Stu! Get up!" I urged, shaking him briskly.

"What's wrong?" he mumbled drowsily.

"Just look at that red sunrise," I replied anxiously, "there's a storm coming!"

"I'm not sure that red in the morning thing is always right," Stu said, slipping out of bed to peer out the window, "but in case it is, we'd better get moving."

We were on our way to Petersburg, and from there south, at the end of our second summer in Saginaw Bay. Old Mac had died the winter after our first summer there and Lois was moving to Kake so it was uncertain what would become of the property. Our own plans were doubtful since we no longer depended entirely on fishing for our livelihood. We thought we might become more interested and involved with our farm in Oregon.

After leaving Saginaw Bay the day before we stopped in Kake to visit friends who operated a small crab cannery a short distance from the native village. We had dinner with Bill and Shirley Short and their children, and spent the night in their vacant cabin with our boat safely tied up at their private dock.

But now we dressed quickly, rolled up our sleeping bags, filled a thermos with coffee and hurried across the road and down the ramp to the boat dock without disturbing our friends.

I paused there a moment, savoring the hush of the early morning. A few birds high in the trees were chirping jubilantly, welcoming the new day. Some small rodent rustled in the brush ashore. The ravens on the beach were carrying on a dialogue, not in their usual noisy croaking, but in low amiable tones as if they too were considerate of the still sleeping world around them.

"Look!" Stu stood gazing at the awesome sight, the violently flaming eastern sky that portended no good. I had never seen a sunrise to equal the wide spread and increasing brilliance.

"Let's get going." A note of urgency in his voice moved us both to action.

Now that we had pulled up our temporary stakes at Saginaw Bay and packed all our belongings aboard we were anxious to get this trip behind us. We had no hankering to sit out the first of the fall equinox storms somewhere on the beach before reaching Petersburg, sixty miles or more to the southeast on Mitkof Island. Our nineteen-foot tri-hulled craft was fast but not large enough to cope with rough seas.

Stu started the motor while I untied the lines. Leaping lightly aboard I gave the boat a shove away from the dock and took my place in the seat opposite his. I was thankful there was no fog this morning as we wound our way between rocks and hidden reefs.

I thought of the early Indians who had built Kake on these rocky shores hoping the unsafe harbor strewn with rocks and dangerous reefs would be protection against their enemies.

Soon the sleeping village was far behind us. The brilliant colors to the east were already fading from the sky but the sun rose a red ball above the tree tops beyond the little cabin. Would we make it before the storm broke?

And, I wondered, would we ever come back to Kake or wind leisurely through the rocky Keku Islands or hear a wolf howl from a desolate bluff overlooking beautiful Saginaw Bay? Was I becoming overly cautious and was the rugged life losing some of its adventurous appeal? In the last few years I had become more reluctant to make the long trips by small boat with possible nights on the beach waiting out a storm.

Rounding Point Macartney into Frederick Sound, the water was smooth, the sky now clearing with almost no ominous signs left to remind us of the sailor's warning.

"How about a cup of coffee?" I asked.

"Sounds good," Stu replied, waving at a passing troller. "He's heading for town too."

Relishing the hot coffee as we skimmed over the still calm

201

blue water, the engine droning steady and smoothly, I thought of the luxury of this small craft compared to the open sixteen-foot boat we used for years. Still, the most fabulous fishing we experienced and some of our most enjoyable years were with the little Reinall, first using a ten horsepower motor and later a twenty-five.

Going to the stern I looked to the left as we sped northeast to round the upper end of Kupreanof Island before turning southeast at Pinta Point. Across Frederick Sound I saw the outline of Admiralty Island and, dimly in the distance, the south end where we spent many satisfying, but not always easy years at Tyee. As the red dawn faded to blue I found time to think. Was it life in the wilderness that was so alluring or meeting the challenge of the elements? Coming to grips with the storms, the treacherous tides, the unpredictable weather and unforeseen hazards — was that what drew us back year after year? Maybe, but there was more, such as the abundant delights nature freely bestowed.

Like the time Stu lured a deer to his side with a deer call made from a piece of willow bough and a rubber band. We were on the beach at the end of Kootznahoo Inlet, both sitting on a low rock. Holding the crude lure to his lips he had made a sort of mewing sound, typical of deer, every minute or so for about ten minutes when suddenly there was a rustling and a small doe stepped out of the brush onto the beach some 200 feet from us. We sat perfectly still, not even blinking and almost stopped breathing when the graceful creature walked cautiously toward us. As Stu carefully continued the mewing without moving, the doe seemed to become more confident or maybe it was responding naturally to a fawn's cry, and it now approached at almost a trot. Reaching the source of the call, she reached out that sleek head with long ears twitching, and sniffed at the sleeve of Stu's jacket. I saw the nostrils quiver, the big beautiful eyes alert. She stood trembling and confused for just a second, then evidently having detected the man smell, snorted, whirled and crashed back into the brush.

Or one late evening in Tyee when we heard loud creaking sounds similar to heavy furniture being dragged across a floor. Walking out on the pier we heard the spouting of whales and noises like nothing we had ever heard before. We listened fascinated while the big creatures moved slowly up the channel. In the near darkness we could see what we thought might have been three or four, their backs showing at intervals above the surface of the water, each about a half length behind the other. After a few minutes they turned and headed back out the channel.

202

The sounds stopped. Later we learned that whales do indeed sing, however harsh and discordant the sound.

"Take a last look at Baranof Island before we go around the point," Stu interrupted my pondering, at the same time slowing down the motor. I followed his gaze back across the straits to the perpetually snow-covered craggy peaks towering over trees and water.

"Remember the summer we stayed at Warm Springs Bay on the Island?"

"And the hot springs baths," I added.

"And the pretty falls," Stu recalled with pleasure, referring to the spectacular falls made by a higher elevation lake spilling over into the salt water bay, creating a scenic picture visible from the window of our cabin.

"Caught a lot of good trout in that lake. Wonder if I'll ever fish it again?" Turning abruptly he bore down on the throttle. "We better keep moving, we have a long way to go yet."

Scanning the skies anxiously I saw scattered clouds appearing in the south and west.

Continuing on around the north end of Kupreanof Island we passed a flock of seagulls, clamoring loudly and swooping down over the water within a small area.

"Must be a small bunch of herring or some other feed there," my husband commented.

"Remember the night we holed up in there?" he asked a few minutes later, pointing to an opening in the jungle-like growth along the shore. I nodded. Unlike the rocky shoreline we were following, the beach here was smooth and sandy.

"Do we dare take time for a quick run in?" Stu questioned, proceeding to turn the boat through the opening into an almost land-locked small cove. The sloping sandy beach was backed by a dense growth of brush and trees, a perfect haven for small craft.

"There's where the young fellows killed the wolf," Stu said, indicating where just before dark we had seen the animal running on the beach. Before it had reached the shelter of the woods a small boat with two young Indians standing up in it had come full speed across the harbor. One of the young men killed the wolf with one shot. Empty now, the pretty little harbor looked lonely but somehow cozy and appealing. I saw a few late wildflowers blooming at the edge of the trees. A mink clambered over some rocks and slithered into the brush.

"That was a nice place to get marooned in," Stu reflected as we left the cove and picked up speed. "Maybe we'll come back some day. But now we've got to keep moving, the storm you were predicting is on our heels," he said, nodding towards the darkening skyline behind us.

I glanced at my husband. Was he too experiencing mixed emotions? There was now the decided attraction of a more comfortable and easy life near the cities in our new home in Oregon. Driving cars, traveling on the big freeways, electric power at our finger tips, the expectation of a telephone call, the chitchat across the fence with close neighbors and not least of all ever-running hot water — all eagerly anticipated pleasures after months in the wilderness. At times I felt my pioneer spirit waning when a balky stove smoked and the wet wood refused to burn; when my back wouldn't unbend after a session at the washboard; or when I was so tired of canned venison I tried to disguise it by every conceivable means.

There were the times when I waited anxiously for Stu, overdue from fishing or hunting by himself. Once I was trying to busy myself in the cabin when I heard the sound of a motor. Quickly I stepped outside expecting to see his boat speeding towards home. But all was silent. As daylight faded I sneaked a glance at the clock every few minutes. Again and again I imagined I heard the motor only to be disappointed when I hurried outdoors. When he finally did come he couldn't understand why I was worried.

"I knew I was all right," he reasoned.

Cruising along smoothly, the water calm, we made good time. Shortly after passing Turnabout Island I saw the coast mountains on the mainland to the east, but they were soon blotted from sight by a sky that was swiftly becoming overcast. I buttoned my jacket against the chill in the now stiff breeze.

More miles sped by, and then a school of porpoises started racing us. Moving carefully to the forward deck, I lay on my stomach and watched them crossing back and forth just inches ahead of the bow. The water was so clear I could see every graceful movement of their lithe, supple bodies.

Back in my seat I remembered the time we were fishing at Tyee and I hooked a baby porpoise. Swiftly it took off. Thinking it was a salmon, Stu started the motor to follow because I didn't have much line left. When we saw larger porpoises following close on each side of the young one, its parents presumably, we realized what had happened and broke the line, releasing the frightened creature. Porpoises are family oriented. An adult will support its dead young on its pectoral fins for some time.

Where else could we live in such close contact with the mysteries of nature? Did I want to give up the slower paced, earthy life of the wilderness? Even the frightening storms had a certain fascination, preferably when witnessed from a cozy cabin. The everyday grappling with the elements was more satisfying than I had ever dreamed. Several black ducks flew up ahead of us, so heavy with feed they could hardly get off the water. Others made no attempt to fly but turned their downy bottoms up as they dived to escape the speeding boat.

Soon we passed the small sandy beach where we had gone ashore on one of our earlier trips. A bush pilot had circled and dipped down to see if we were in trouble. Stu signalled all was well.

An hour later we passed Portage Bay, the last good harbor before reaching Petersburg. Our sense of urgency seemed to lessen as we neared the end of this leg of our journey. Maybe the red sunrise wasn't a threat. Then I noticed fast moving darker clouds low on the horizon. The water had turned lead gray.

"There are the last two little islands, not much farther to go," Stu observed with a reassuring pat on my shoulder. "We won't forget this trip, just one jump ahead of the storm."

"Won't be long now," I added with relief. Soon we'd be in the city. However small, there were sidewalks, stores, people and cafés. For the first time in months I wouldn't be eating my own cooking or washing the dishes, at least not until we were back in Oregon.

Before entering Wrangell Narrows, the entrance to Petersburg, Stu released the throttle, letting the boat drift while he stood gazing about.

"There's Kate's Needle," he said, pointing to a sharp jagged mountain peak in the far distance across Frederick Sound, visible for just a moment before the threatening clouds hid it from view.

"Look at that ice." I gestured towards huge chunks that had broken off Le Conte Glacier and floated with the tide out into the middle of the sound. "More than I ever saw here before." The miniature icebergs were not large enough to be a hazard to large boats, but submerged pieces could be dangerous for small craft after dark. We stayed at a safe distance knowing a small boat could be swamped by a chunk shifting or turning over. Several trolling boats were scattered across the now choppy water. Two or three small skiffs moved along the shore all headed towards the harbor. Everywhere the evergreen shores were heavily wooded.

What was my husband thinking? Slowly he turned. "Do you think we'll come back again?" he asked, searching my face.

"I'm sure we will," I replied with more confidence than I felt.

"Look! Whales! Over there," I exclaimed pointing to several dark backs surfacing in close succession.

"Want to chase them?" Stu asked pointedly.

"Not this time," I smiled, remembering. "We'd best get in before the storm hits."

He motioned toward the southwest. The lowering clouds were closing in. A sudden gust of wind stirred the darkening water.

Moments later we were bouncing through the swift and turbulent currents into Wrangell Narrows.

"Nice to see real homes again," I thought, watching children and dogs playing in the yards along the channel.

"We didn't get here any too soon," Stu declared, when we finally tied up in the small boat harbor. "It's going to be a helluva blow." Although the harbor was in a well protected basin, fishermen were scurrying about securing loose articles, closing hatches and taking extra precautions against the menacing weather.

Before we had finished carrying our luggage to a hotel, the wind was blowing a gale, and the rain beat slantwise against our faces. When everything was safely inside we removed our dripping slickers and tidied up a bit.

"Now, let's go have a big steak," Stu said cheerfully and taking my hand we dashed across the street to a neon café sign.

Furiously the storm pounded most of southeastern Alaska for three days. We ventured out in the deluge only to eat and check the boat. Violent gusts of wind and rain rattled the windows and beat against the sturdy little hotel while we listened on the radio to Coast Guard reports of boats floundering in the angry seas.

"Had we been an hour or two later coming in, we'd be sitting out there on the beach somewhere now," Stu said, voicing what was also on my mind. I shivered. Alaska and the storms that were a part of it was not at all attractive to me right now.

"What will we do with the boat?" I asked.

"Put it in storage again," Stu answered. Ever since we had gotten the new boat we had stored it for the winters in a construction contractor's big barn where he kept equipment.

"I'll make arrangements to have it shipped down if we don't come back," he added. I looked at him quietly but I was thinking, "That's the first time in all these years I've heard an 'if.'"

With the gale over and our boat safely in storage we boarded the ferry late one night. Standing on the aft deck as it glided southward through Wrangell Narrows, we watched the lights of Petersburg disappear in the distance. Here and there a solitary light from a home glowed dimly in the darkness. Only the low rumble of the ferry engines and the rippling of water from the wake broke the midnight silence.

Just as we turned to go inside my husband grasped my arm. "Look! The Northern Lights!"

We lingered to watch the shimmering bands of light like colorful draperies fluttering from the heavens. Not the flaming beauty of the red sunrise that spurred us to action a few days earlier, but a softer, more awesome beauty from the mysterious phenomenon that quiets the soul like a solemn benediction.

Come spring, with the sight and sound of wild geese flying north and the persistent drumlike call of the hooter grouse, I knew we would again both feel a definite "listing to the north."